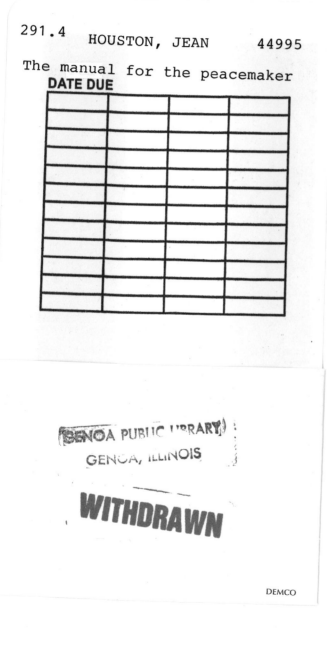

MANUAL

FOR THE

PEACEMAKER

©John D. Dove, May, 1994

MANUAL
FOR THE

PEACEMAKER

AN IROQUOIS LEGEND
TO HEAL SELF & SOCIETY

BY JEAN HOUSTON
WITH MARGARET RUBIN

QUEST BOOKS
The Theosophical Publishing House
Wheaton, IL U.S.A.
Madras, India/London, England

The Theosophical Publishing House
P.O. Box 270
Wheaton, IL 60189-0270

A publication of the Theosophical Publishing House,
a department of the Theosophical Society in America.

*This publication made possible with
the assistance of the Kern Foundation.*

Library of Congress Cataloging-in-Publication Data

Houston, Jean.
    Manual for the peacemaker : an Iroquois legend to heal self & society / Jean
Houston with Margaret Rubin.
    p. cm.
    Includes bibliographical references (p. 173).
    ISBN 0-8356-0709-7
    ISBN 0-8356-0735-6-(Tradepaper)
    1. Shamanism. 2. Centering (Psychology)—Miscellanea. 3. Imagery
(Psychology)—Miscellanea. 4. Iroquois Indians—Legends. 5. Indians of North
America—Legends. I. Rubin, Margaret Nash. II. Title.
BF1611.H68 1994   94-37906
291.4'4—dc20   CIP

9 8 7 6 5 4 3 2 1 * 95 96 97 98 99

This edition is printed on acid-free paper that meets the
American National Standards Institute Z39.48 Standard

For the Peacemakers

CONTENTS

▲▲▲

ACKNOWLEDGMENTS

There are many who have contributed to the inspiration of this book, most particularly my many friends and teachers of the First Nation, the original inhabitants of this land. Among these are the late Mad Bear Anderson, himself a leader among the Iroquois people, who first introduced me to the story of the creation of the League of the Haudenosaunee; Wub-e-ke-niew (Francis Blake) and Clara Niiska of the Anishinabe Ojibway nation; Loretta Afraid-of-Bear Cook of the Oglala Sioux. From the non-Native teachers I wish to salute the beautiful teachings of Sea Dancer (Diane Battung), who has embraced the Native traditions with honor, respect, and deep love. She has taught me much. Emmy Devine, our divine teacher of sacred dance at Mystery School, offered her wealth of knowledge gleaned from many years of studies with Native American teachers.

Again, as with many other books, Elisabeth Zinck Rothenberger has lovingly transcribed the original presentation of this material as it was given in Mystery School. William Bryant provided us with valuable sources, suggestions, and corrections for the original material.

I want to especially thank my Quest editor Brenda Rosen for her tireless efforts and dedication to the development and editing of this manuscript.

My colleague Margaret Nash Rubin contributed so richly to the creation of the seminars that became the basis for this book, as well as adding much to the research and writing, that I thought it appropriate that she share the authorship.

How To Use
This Book

This book is intended to enable groups of people to experience together the transformational power of one of the greatest stories ever told. In the pages that follow, you will enter the story of Deganawidah and Hiawatha, following the stages of their creation of a New Peace and a New Mind and, in so doing, experience your own potential for renewing both self and society. The notes that follow are offered as guidelines for making these sessions all that they can be. They are similar to preparatory notes that I offer in my other books dealing with transformational journeys. The group that meets together to experience these exercises must devote careful attention to the preparation and conducting of these sessions. Included also are recommendations for those who will be journeying alone.

The Nature of the Group

As the import of these experiences can be trivial or profound, it is necessary that the intention of the group and of its members be clear from the beginning. The group should consist only of those who freely choose to participate and who feel well motivated to do so. The community that composes the members of the group may take any form: family, friends, colleagues, students, clients, parishioners, and so forth. In general, the experiences should be undertaken by intelligent, resourceful people who have had sufficient life experience to appreciate the historical and psychological scope of the human and social drama they will be required to go through.

Working in groups helps to eradicate one of the worst tyrannies that afflicts Homo sapiens—the tyranny of the dominant perception. This is reflected in such statements as "If it's good enough for me, it's good enough for you" and "Why can't you respond like everyone else does?" The participants in each of the exercises that grow out of this extraordinary story will stimulate, support, and evoke each other. In their diverse reactions, they will prime a diversity of responses within and among themselves. While consensus and commonalties are important, our differences are equally enriching: "Thank God," we say to ourselves, "I need not be limited to my own experience but may share in yours." As we recognize the enormous richness of experience in others, we drop simplistic judgments and projections and stand in awe before the wild abundance of human variation.

By pursuing the adventures that form the Manual for the Peacemaker as part of a group, we also bypass one of the most insidious of human failings—the potential for sloth. Self-discipline and good intentions have a way of evaporating without some consistent external support. The practices and procedures in this book challenge deeply entrenched patterns of mind, body, and psyche, and thus allies are needed to help us remount the slope of thought and acquire new ways of being. Resistance to change is natural, maybe even healthy, but one of the few ways to overcome it is through regular participation in the mutually helpful, empowering, and celebrating company of fellow journeyers. This is why those who are voyaging alone need to tell at least one person close to them of their undertaking.

The group of voyagers should probably number not fewer than five nor more than twenty-five, although I have conducted groups of over 150 through similar processes. There should also be an odd number of participants, since some of the experiences are performed by couples while one member of the group is acting as Guide.

At its initial meeting the group should assign members to take responsibility for obtaining and preparing the setting or settings (indoors or out) for each of the exercises. This includes providing appropriate music and record, tape, or CD players; art and craft supplies; drums, flutes, rattles; paper, drawing and other art materials; as well as food for closing celebrations after each exercise. Special

attention must be taken that during the sessions there be no intrud-
ers, wandering dogs, curious children, or ringing telephones. (Let me
modify that. Wandering dogs have often played a welcome role in
many of my seminars and have become much loved members of all
of my Mystery School sessions. Also, virtually all Native American
ceremonials and councils I have witnessed were also attended by
visiting dogs. Generally, dogs know how to act appropriately and
provide needed affection and wordless understanding.) The setting
is to be treated as sacred space. In fact, it is a good idea to begin
each session by burning sage or Native American sweetgrass sticks.
This practice purifies the atmosphere and provides holy smoke to
remind us that we are in sacred time and space.

Prior to each meeting every member of the group should read the
relevant material in this book. The text should be read in such a way
that the reader dialogues with it, taking note of images and ideas
that emerge so that these may feed the group discussion. The group
discussion of this material should in most cases be the first part
of the group's meeting, its purpose being to explore the meaning
of the story in the lives and understanding of the members. The
intention of the discussion is to evoke a depth sensibility of historical,
social, mythic, and personal patterns, not to describe and dissect
each participant's life and times. Another part of the discussion
session (which can be led by a member of the group or by the Guide)
might be devoted to a sharing of reflections concerning the changing
patterns of viewpoint and awareness that members have observed
in themselves since the last meeting. Many have found it extremely
valuable to keep a journal of their experiences, often decorating the
cover of their journals with images or drawings that evokes both the
spirit and content of their personal journey.

After the discussion has ended, there should be a break of at least
fifteen minutes before the group comes back together to share the
experiences of the particular stage of the story of Deganawidah
and Hiawatha. A good way to do this is to leave the space in
which the discussion was held and reenter it after a while as sacred
space, silently, with full awareness of a commitment to making the
exercise meaningful. Each member of the group will spend some time
centering and bringing his or her consciousness to an awareness of

the experiences about to unfold. Each should make a kind of internal commitment to take responsibility for his or her own personal experience and, at the same time, be respectful of the needs of others and of the group as a whole.

THE GUIDE

Ideally the Guide is a person who has already participated in similar transformational processes with another group, though this need not be the case. At the initial preparatory meeting, the group will decide who the Guide or Guides will be and how they will function. The Guide can be the same for all sessions, or the role can rotate. The groups that form to explore the Manual for the Peacemaker must avoid the error: Guide equals leader. The Guide should be understood by everyone to be one who assists, one who enables. As enabler, the Guide serves the needs of the voyage into sacred psychology and of the voyagers.

The Guide will prepare for the session by reading the relevant material in the text with great care and, whenever possible, will do extra reading about Native American society and beliefs as suggested by the bibliography at the end of this book. Also, prior to each exercise, the Guide will engage in a period of relaxation, deep breathing, and meditation. Listening to Native American flute music, such as the recordings listed in the Musical Selections section, may aid the meditation. The Guide might also try drumming with a steady beat to enhance the meditation. The goal of the meditation is to become conscious of and to eliminate ego hungers and power drives, as well as any other improper attitudes or tendencies that would be exploitative or manipulative of the voyagers. It must be remembered that the role of the Guide is a most ancient one, found in one of its most accomplished forms in the hierophants of the ancient Mysteries. In the tradition taught here, the Guide is the midwife of souls, the evocator of growth and transformation. In becoming Guide, then, one knows oneself to be part of a continuity stretching across millennia. It is a role of the greatest challenge and responsibility, and one invests it, therefore, with High Self.

The Guide needs to have the capacity to be at once part of the experience and observer of the voyage of the travelers. She, or he, must be able to judge sensitively the amount of time needed for each part of the journey and to use the experiences flexibly. The experiences described are not cast in stone and would probably gain much from the suggestions and additions of the group and the Guide.

The Guide will have read the exercise materials aloud several times before the group meeting, sensing the nature of the journey and allowing his or her voice and timing to reflect that experience. The Guide will note that a series of dots (. . .) in a process script means that time must be given for the participants to follow and experience the suggestions given. The Guide's voice must not be intrusive, lugubrious, or overly dramatic, but must remain clear and appropriate to the experience. Wherever music is part of the process, the Guide must rehearse so as to integrate carefully the timing of the reading and the music.

The Guide will always have one or more "soul catchers" present. These are members of the group selected because of their ability to be sensitive to the needs of others. Thus, even while going through the experiences themselves, they will have a part of their consciousness available to help others should this be required. It must be stated, however, that part of helping others may be in knowing when to let someone alone and not intrude unnecessarily on his or her experience. The soul catcher will also have the task of guiding the Guide through the process shortly after the group journey has ended, if the Guide so desires.

TREADING GENTLY

In working with this material, it is most important that members of the group refrain from acting as therapists or theologians. Professional therapists and theologians may find this very difficult, but it is imperative that they practice their profession only during regular working hours. Comments I have heard, despite repeated pleas to refrain from making them, have included, "You really are blocked,"

"I can see some enormous anger stored up there," and even "You clearly are spiritually immature." Such remarks are inappropriate here even if they seem accurate and you intend them to be helpful. Acceptance of people for who and what they are in the present moment is critical to the practice of sacred psychology. Each person is perfectly capable of interpreting his or her own experience and can invite the comments of others if desired.

One of the great advantages of sacred psychology is that it invites the participant to move into high witness, to tap into forgotten wisdom, and to practice nonobtrusive spiritual intimacy with others. One is always in a place to see the other as God-in-hiding, and to be so seen oneself. Many of the processes given in this book allow for the practice of deep empathy maintained in a variety of ways—the gentle holding of the hand of your partner while she or he is describing experience or reflections; eye-to-eye contact whenever appropriate; and, above all, careful and compassionate listening that knows when to speak out of one's deepest wisdom and when to maintain silence, communicating understanding and respect by eye or gesture alone. The sharing of powerful experience and reflection that accompanies the processes of this book especially when done by a group requires that people enter into a state of mutual trust. Thus after sharing an experience with a partner, I have found it to be a good and satisfying thing to express words of appreciation to each other for the trust given. One might say, for example, "I am honored that you shared so deeply of your experience with me."

Please, please, keep in mind that there is no such thing as doing any exercise wrong. This is a journey of the soul, and each person will have his or her unique way of approaching it. In fact, whenever possible, BE INVENTIVE! Do the exercise differently, or add other ideas or images or actions with which to enhance the process.

TIME AND SPACE AND THE PLACES IN BETWEEN

The set of exercises in the Manual for the Peacemaker can be performed over different time periods—even over the period of a very long day, although some have found this too compacted and intense. Others, however, have found a condensed sequence extremely powerful for the immediate continuity it provides for all stages in the story of Deganawidah and Hiawatha. A two- to three-day period, like a weekend, is perhaps the best time period within which to enter and experience the stages of the Manual for the Peacemaker. Initially, however, one might do well to have a preparatory meeting in which the group assigns responsibilities and chooses the Guide or Guides. This is followed by the weekend meeting in which the entire sequence of exercise and discussion is experienced. It is extremely important that each member of the group make a firm commitment to the other members to be on time and to see the entire sequence through to its completion. To leave it suddenly is to open oneself to further fissures and frustrations in attempting the creation of a New Mind and a New Peace. Completed, however, the entire process has proved to be a most potent and revealing therapy, providing the orchestral dynamics with which to integrate the structures of one's being with the energy and genius of Native American knowings. What emerges is the possible human as a living reality, ready and willing to help in the development of a more possible society.

IF YOU ARE JOURNEYING ALONE

If you are entering the Manual for the Peacemaker by yourself, you need to make a serious commitment to engage in and complete all of the processes. Thus, it seems important that you perform whatever are your most effective modes or rituals of preparation. Buy a new notebook for journaling. Make sure you have art materials for drawing, pens and pencils for writing. Create a special sacred space where you will work; it is best if this space has a boundary of some kind, so that you cross a threshold to enter it. This prevents the energies of everyday life from bleeding through and diverting your attention.

Make sure there is music available for you there—your favorites as well as the Native American music suggested at the end of this book.

Set specific times for doing this work. As journeying solo can be more challenging than journeying with a group, it probably is not advisable to attempt to complete the stages of this journey during the course of a long weekend. If you decide to do this work on a weekly basis, then make an agreement with yourself about those times; try not to let more than a week go by between sessions. Dedicate that time to complete immersion within the process from the story of Deganawidah and Hiawatha which you are entering.

You may wish to decorate the front of your journal with appropriate images. If it seems helpful, you might even decorate your space and wear clothes specially chosen for this story.

Write out a contract with yourself to embark upon this journey through sacred psychology and to complete it. Set the time span that you allow yourself for the entire sequence. Sign and date the contract. You might even wish to set a forfeit should you not comply with the terms of the contract. This could be giving up for a time special foods or entertainments that you enjoy or, on a more constructive note, giving a service to friends or community, offering unexpected help to surprise and delight.

Then tell someone who cares about you and will support your inner work that you're making a transformational journey. Ask if you may call upon this person occasionally to ask for assistance, a second opinion, or a shoulder to lean on. Have this friend witness and sign the contract you have made.

In my experience it has proven to be good practice to work with at least one other person in making this journey. Another voice, another life story, a companion for the road helps train us in that most valuable of human skills—working, playing, and growing together with mutual regard and care. I realize that, for many people, this is not easy or practical. But at least tell someone what you're doing, and invite your ally to participate in the process by seeing that you keep your side of the bargain.

The most important thing that you have to do in voyaging solo is to prerecord the scripts for the Guide on tape. This will give you greater freedom and spontaneity in doing the exercises. A cautionary note here. Please do not use an overly dramatic or peculiar voice when you make the tapes, or you'll end up not trusting the person on the tape! Also, be sure to leave yourself pauses of sufficient length wherever they're called for so that you have enough time to do the exercises properly.

Where processes require working with other people, there are suggestions at appropriate places in the text for solo journeyers. But, as a general rule, using your imagination is key. Wherever a partner or partners are needed, you can imagine or visualize them being present and then enact the interaction and/or dialogue with them by writing in your journal. In fact, try to create an ongoing process of dialogue, interchange, and persuasion by devising new ways of working with your journal. It is a marvelous thing to experience yourself as a participant in a great and fruitful life. Record the images and feelings that will inevitably come of this experience. Create, if you can, art with your learning and your feelings. Write poetry, draw and paint, work in clay and other materials. Do Native American crafts, work with shells and beads, carve images in wood and, above all, drum. It makes no difference whether you think you have a special gift for writing or for crafts; just let your imagination loose. Free your hand to move as it wants, directed by your inner knowing and seeing. You may be surprised and pleased with the results. You may also wish to burn sage or sweetgrass at the beginning of the session, to purify the surroundings and to create the appropriate atmosphere for inner work and sacred ceremony.

LET US BEGIN THE JOURNEY

Thus warned and primed, let us begin. We are about to take a depth experiential look at one of the greatest stories and teachings to come from the American shores. To participate in the story of Deganawidah and Hiawatha and the creation of the Iroquois Confederacy is to experience the possibility of the creation of the possible human and the possible society and to learn some of the steps and procedures that we, too, can use to make this dream a manifest reality.

An ancient Tewa Indian prayer speaks to the mending of the earth and the greening of the mind that reflects the principles found in the Manual for the Peacemaker. Its words are: "Within and around the earth, within and around the hills, within and around the mountain, your authority returns to you."

To the earth, the hills, the mountain we offer this reflection of a great story.

INTRODUCTION

▲▲▲

This book invites you to participate in a legend about a bringer of peace, a creator of community, a changer of his world. It is one of the richest stories to come out of North America, yet for non-Native Americans, it is one of the least known. It tells of Deganawidah, the Man from the North, celebrated even today as the Peacemaker, and his successful campaign to create a peaceful and prosperous society, where previously there had been only long years of violence and intertribal warfare. So potent is this legend, so full of pith and wonder, that it embodies the essence of myth, yet many of its elements are acknowledged as historical truths. For Deganawidah actually lived and worked in ways both mythical and practical. His allies included Jigonhsasee, remembered as the Mother of Nations, and the great orator Hayenwatha, remembered as Hiawatha. Together they created a peaceful democracy among five tribes of Native peoples in the northeastern woodlands, a true democracy that lasted hundreds of years and is still, to a remarkable extent, in force today. European settlers gave this nation the name Iroquois; they call themselves the Haudenosaunee, the People of the Longhouse.

The figure of Deganawidah carries archetypal power as a new kind of Peacemaker; his peace embraces what he calls a New Mind, a radical change in consciousness that opens itself to a new order of health, justice, and sacred power. Thus the peace that he proposes is vigorous and demanding, rigorous and challenging. He does not arrive from on high with answers spelled out and a completed plan; though he knows himself to be a messenger of the Great Spirit, he invites others to help him clarify the message and carry it forward persuasively to kin and kind. As his mission proceeds, so does the peace, becoming feisty and rich! It is peace expressed through dynamic conversation, intensive sharing of ideas, ceremony, and cooperation; peace that appeals to all levels of human experience: physical, psychological, mythic, and spiritual.

I believe that Deganawidah deserves to be as well known as other originators of people-centered government. He helped establish a complex and comprehensive democracy in America long before the Colonists arrived. Proofs of this achievement and stories about him were carried back to Europe by the earliest settlers, soldiers, traders, and missionary priests, and these stories influenced many of the seminal thinkers of England and France who promoted the ideals of a democratic society. As Felix Cohen has written, "Politically, there was nothing in the Empires and kingdoms of Europe in the fifteenth and sixteenth centuries to parallel the democratic constitution of the Iroquois Confederacy, with its provisions for initiative, referendum and recall, and its suffrages for women as well as for men."[1] Included too in this democratic tradition were the pattern of states within an embracing State and the practice of chiefs being always the accountable servants of the people, never the lords. Religious freedom, as well as the liberty to follow one's own beliefs and dreams, were a given to the Native peoples and stood in sharp contrast to the rigid demands of Church and State known by most Europeans.

These radical and innovative ideas found their way to Europe quite early, influencing Thomas More and the vision of an optimal society he expressed in *Utopia*. Later, "to John Locke, the champion of tolerance and the right of revolution, the state of nature and of natural equality to which men might appeal in rebellion against tyranny was set not in the remote dawn of history, but beyond the Atlantic sunset."[2] There is much evidence to suggest that the Indian influence extended to the great social theorists of the Enlightenment, among them Montesquieu, Rousseau, and Voltaire. Thus the great ideas and models of democracy began in America with the Native population, crossed the Atlantic to simmer in Europe, and were reimported back to these shores to inform and encourage the Founding Fathers.

They in turn were further inspired by their direct contact with the councils of the Iroquois Confederacy. They adapted freely the ideals and procedures of the Native confederacy and their councils, along with many of their symbols, incorporating these into the governance of the infant republic. As Bruce Johansen reminds us, "a republic existed on our soil before anyone here had ever heard of John Locke, or Cato, or the Magna Carta, Rousseau, Franklin or Jefferson."[3]

It was Benjamin Franklin who did more than anyone else to promote the genius of the Iroquois League and recommend the adoption of many of its practices. As printer and publisher of the *Pennsylvania Gazette*, he regularly offered reports of the Indian treaty councils, beginning as early as 1736. At one council held in Lancaster, Pennsylvania, in 1744, to forge an alliance between the English colonists and the Iroquois to stop the French advancement, an Onondaga chief, Canassatego, a man of booming voice and commanding presence, counseled the Colonists to unite just as the tribes of the Iroquois had done in Deganawidah's day. "Brethren," he is remembered as saying, "We the Six Nations heartily recommend Union and a good agreement between you and our Brethren, never disagree but preserve a strict Friendship, for one another and thereby you as well as we will become stronger. Our Wise Forefathers established Unity and Amity between the Five Nations . . . we are a powerful Confederacy, and if you observe the same methods . . . you will acquire fresh strength and power."[4]

Ten years later at the Albany Congress, Franklin, influenced by Canassatego, proposed a plan to unite the Colonies which followed closely upon the ideals and organization of the Iroquois League. Although not accepted at the time, the Albany plan became a major influence twenty years later in the Articles of Confederation and was key in the creation of the Constitution and formation of the young republic. Franklin himself never stopped talking and writing about the Iroquois League and the great benefit that would come to any burgeoning democracy by following its principles. His persuasive influence on Thomas Jefferson, James Madison, John Adams, and other framers of the Constitution was considerable, as it also was on his friends and devotees in France, some of whom were inspired to consider an end to the monarchy there and the creation of a new republic along principles inspired by the Iroquois.

For this and much more, Deganawidah, the Man from the North, is entitled to be acknowledged as root and inspiration for many of the democracies of the world and, in fact, for many of the responsive and responsible movements to bring about peace with justice, health, and spiritual power. Equally important for us today, his work provides a model for the creation of dynamic communities within a possible world community, especially for a world that is emerging from a century unparalleled for carnage, holocaust, inequities, and political, ethnic, and religious strife. And because the story seems so old that it has the impact of a great myth, we can explore it for its meaning today without ever coming to an end, or without ever being able to say, "This, and this only, is what it means."

Why is Deganawidah the Peacemaker not better known? For that matter, why is it only recently that scholars are admitting the enormous debt that the creation of the American republic owes to Native example and inspiration—so much so that it can truly be said that it was the Indians who taught the European settlers how to be Americans? One reason may be that it seems impossible for a conqueror to acknowledge the debts of gratitude he owes to the people he has conquered. In the case of the European conquerors of North America, there has been no payment made for lands and rights, no treaties kept, few kindnesses given for many kindnesses received—only disease, war, racism, and the desire to see the original people of this country totally extinguished. Certainly there have been humane exceptions to the litany of our cruelty to the Native populations, but they are dwarfed by the harsh realities of conquest and genocide, the refusal of sovereignty and the betrayal of treaties, policies that remained, and still remain, part of our official stance. Perhaps the wrongs we have inflicted are so stunning that we are literally incapable of taking them in, and so we shut them out and make ourselves blind and deaf to the consequences of our prejudices in action. Or we declare, often enough to persuade ourselves that it is true, that we were really bringing the great gift of civilization to the "uncivilized."

Yet we of the "civilized" West have brought the world to the edge of ecological disaster, and perhaps it is only by learning humbly what the aboriginal peoples can teach us about relating to each other and to our earth that we have any hope of real change. These peoples hold a knowing that invites true reason and yet exceeds all rational discourse; they can access the great connection between mind and nature that brings us home to our true place in the order of things. Thus the tremendous interest in learning about and following Native American paths and spirituality. Thus, too, the writing of this book and the story of the mission, the teachings, and the accomplishments of the Peacemaker Deganawidah.

Given this, we find ourselves on the horns of an agonizing dilemma: to deliver this message is to write about a story that is not "ours," that will be said to have been "stolen" from the very people we wish to honor, and to commit again an act that will be construed as everything from political incorrectness at the least, to another appropriation of the cherished and precious material belonging to a population which we have done our best to destroy.

That view acknowledged, we say also that Deganawidah and Hiawatha are models stringently needed today, and if the news of their work can be spread even a little more widely through this book, then that is reason enough for this book to be written.

HOW I HEARD THE STORY

The historical story of the founding of the Iroquois Confederacy of five Indian nations by Deganawidah and Hiawatha and their allies probably took place between 1000 and 1500 A.D., depending on the methods used to estimate the time. Over the years, the story itself has been embroidered upon and elaborated in many versions. For this book, I have pieced together aspects of different narratives from numerous sources, including accounts from Iroquois elders. The first person who recounted it to me was the Tuscarora wisdom keeper, Mad Bear Anderson, and the circumstances of his telling revealed the true spirit of the Peacemaker.

Back in 1975, I chaired a week-long conference of the world's religious leaders, called to celebrate the thirtieth anniversary of the founding of the United Nations. The meeting was a joint effort of the U.N. and the Temple of Understanding, an ecumenical organization that fostered dialogue among religions. The plan was to bring together for the first time, under the auspices of the U.N., those who carried the brief for the human spirit with those who held the file on the human race. It was hoped that religious leaders and U.N. officials would speak long and deeply to each other, sharing ideas, information, and perspectives.

We invited seven spiritual leaders of Native American tribes to be part of the formal conference, but two hundred American Indians showed up, because the keeper of the Hopi prophecy, Grandpa David Mononge, a wise and much revered man, 105 years old, had received a vision that they were all to travel to the tall glass house on the river where they, as citizens of the First Nation, would be recognized for the first time by all nations.

I asked some of the Native elders to define their role at the conference. This was my first meeting with Mad Bear Anderson, a Tuscarora leader from the Iroquois nation of upstate New York, who answered my question wonderfully well: "The Eastern religions represent spirituality that looks inward. The Western religions represent spirituality that tends to look outward. We are the people whose spirituality is of the middle. We stand for the sacrality of Nature, for the sacred ways of the Earth. Therefore, we can be mediators between East and West, reminding the others that Nature is holy and full of the Great Spirit."

"But, Mad Bear," I asked, "what shall I do with all of you? There are so many of you that there will not be enough room for the representatives of the other religions, let alone the U.N. officials, if we fill each meeting room with your people."

"We will go into council now and elect representatives, for that is our way."

And that is what they did. In each of the meeting rooms with an assigned group of religious leaders balanced between East and West, it was these Native Americans who listened most deeply to the issues of nation and spirit. They then provided the most penetrating reflections on the profound choices we all had to make together if the earth and its peoples were to continue. After each meeting the

Native representative would go back and discuss the content of the session with all the others, so that all felt that they had been a part.

As for food and housing (for two hundred, when we had planned for seven, a detail which worried me extremely), the group relished the gourmet meals provided by the conference—"as good as bear claws," one Onondaga elder laughed, while chewing lustily on Beef Wellington. As for lodging, the Reverend Miyake, a wealthy Japanese Shinto priest, put all the Native Americans up in New York's Waldorf Astoria. We all enjoyed seeing them clothed in traditional dress holding Pow Wows each morning in the lobby, under the crystal chandeliers.

So richly appreciated was the Native American contribution to the conference that they were invited to take on nongovernmental organization status. They did so, setting up an office near the U.N. and subsequently joining other international organizations for First Nation peoples.

So balanced and reasonable had been the Native American contribution at this event, so deep, eloquent, and healing their reflections, that I asked Mad Bear to explain the secret of their wisdom and equanimity. "There is no secret," he replied. "It is simply that many of us try to follow the example that the Peacemaker set for us so long ago." Then he proceeded to tell me something of the story that I tell in this book.

As Mad Bear related the legend and the teachings of the Peacemaker, I felt as if I were being initiated into some great community of hearers who transcended time and place, tribe or nation. There was sacred power in the story; its words were doors that opened upon a possible world and gave one the means to inhabit that world. The telling became part of my bones, and I continued over the years to seek it in many different variations as well as in many books and records. The fact that it was history as well as myth gave it both moral and spiritual authority. For it is a soul-charging tale, one that is rich in the details of how to create an ideal society: a society that is peaceful and prosperous, as well as democratic; a society that addresses the spiritual and psychological as well as the economic and political needs of humankind; a society that speaks to universal suffrage, to partnership between men and women, and, indeed, to cooperation between all nations; a society that fosters and promotes peace as a living dynamic entity. I believe that this great story can serve as a greening guidance, a tree of light, within whose branches we may begin to find the patterns and the strength for our own present renewal of self and society.

I have referred many times in my seminars and books to the state of whole system transition in which we live, a time in which literally everything is changing so rapidly and completely that we are in a jump phase in history, an open moment in which what we do profoundly makes a difference for good or for ill. In such open moments, the very best and the very worst rise to meet us. As William Butler Yeats expressed it in his great poem, "The Second Coming": "Things fall apart; the center cannot hold; Mere anarchy is loosed upon the world, . . . The best lack all conviction, while the worst/Are full of passionate intensity."

The Deganawidah story is about such a time of utter breakdown, continuous savagery, and warfare. But unlike the "rough beast" of Yeats' poem, which in the open moment, "slouches towards Bethlehem to be born," Deganawidah comes on the scene filled with the spirit of the Peacemaker. Like many another savior figure, he is born of a virgin; threatened with death as a baby; grows up misunderstood and an outcast; is thoughtful and wise and remarkable but not appreciated by his own tribe; goes out to other tribes; and preaches a gospel not just of peace, but of New Mind and new power, of a new order of community and justice, health and creativity. The message is accepted by some, rejected by others. People are desperate for a new message because this is a time in which the world is a wasteland, savaged by war.

WILL THE REAL HIAWATHA PLEASE STEP FORWARD?

Deganawidah needs a helper, and he chooses an Onondaga tribal leader who has been driven mad by the suffering and torment in which he lives. Many of his children and his wife have been killed, and he has become a cannibal. This savage man, who later comes to be called Hiawatha, is cured of his cannibalism through the magic of goodness and forgiveness and then returns to his people to help save the mind, body, and soul of the most twisted and corrupted member of his society, the sorcerer Tadodaho. The legend also tells how Hiawatha became the spokesman for Deganawidah, who, like Moses, could not talk very clearly.

Many people have an entirely different set of associations with Hiawatha, thanks to Henry Wadsworth Longfellow. His epic poem, *The Song of Hiawatha*, is about another tribe and another person: the fabulous, semimythic hero of the Ojibway whose real name is Manabozho (sometimes known as Nanabozho). Longfellow's source for his poem had confused the two: In the middle 1800s, Henry Rowe Schoolcraft had gathered notes about both the Ojibway and the Iroquois tribal heroes and written a book, *The Hiawatha Legends,* describing the actions of Manabozho, but identifying him as Hiawatha.

While Longfellow's poem tells a different tale than the one we are unfolding, it nevertheless speaks in soaring verse of how legendary stories encode the renewal of our personal and our public life and of how the Great Spirit (that is, Gitche Manito among the Natives of the Great Lakes region, Wakan Tanka of the Plains People, Akee of the Iroquois people) rises to inform this renewal in times of trouble. It speaks to the conditions of war and combat that were prevalent in Deganawidah's time as well as in our own.

I invite you to speak aloud these words from Longfellow's poem, and imagine that you hear a drumbeat behind the words:

> Ye who love a nation's legends,
> Love the ballads of a people,
> That like voices from afar off
> Call to us to pause and listen,
> Speak in tones so plain and childlike,
> Scarcely can the ear distinguish
> Whether they are sung or spoken;

Listen to this Indian Legend,
To this Song of Hiawatha!

Gitche Manito, the mighty,
The Creator of the nations,
Looked upon them with compassion,
With paternal love and pity; . . .
    "O my children! my poor children!
Listen to the words of wisdom,
Listen to the words of warning,
From the lips of the Great Spirit,
From the Master of Life, who made you!
    "I have given you lands to hunt in,
I have given you streams to fish in,
I have given you bear and bison,
I have given you roe and reindeer,
I have given you brant and beaver,
Filled the marshes full of wild-fowl,
Filled the rivers full of fishes,
Why then are you not contented?
Why then will you hunt each other?
    "I am weary of your quarrels,
Weary of your wars and bloodshed,
Weary of your prayers for vengeance,
Of your wranglings and dissensions;
All your strength is in your union,
All your danger is in discord;
Therefore be at peace henceforward,
And as brothers live together . . ."

Carrying a message not unlike the one Longfellow expressed here,
Deganawidah and Hiawatha, along with an early convert, Jigonhsasee, the Mother of Nations, brought together warring tribes in such
a way as to create the basis of a new society. Composed of five
nations—the Mohawk, Seneca, Cayuga, Oneida, and Onondaga—
this new society became a League of five nations, known as the

Haudenosaunee or Iroqouis Confederacy. Later, in the early eighteenth century, the League added a sixth nation, the Tuscarora.

A New Story for Then and for Now

The tale of Deganawidah also speaks radically to the open moment we live in, a time in which anarchy, dissolution, and lack of guidance and leadership have made us so full of holes that we've become holy. As a result, many people all over the world have become available to their depths in ways that happen only a few times in human history. An open moment is a time when literally everything is up for grabs or up for destruction, or both. Because of its interweaving of myth and history, we find in the Deganawidah legend an analogue to our own experience. Most of us have survived ten to a hundred times the amount of experience of our ancestors of, say, a hundred and fifty years ago. As a result, we are much more fragmented and wounded than our forebears. Living as we do in times of utter and overwhelming transformation at every level of life, we, unlike our ancestors, came into life without givens. Thus we have the disadvantage (or the advantage, depending on how you look at it) of needing to create a new story for ourselves and our world. This task has made us mythic, inhabiting the same twilight world between history and legend in which the Deganawidah story takes place. Perhaps it is because our time is so similar to his that the tale of Deganawidah is arising again today.

In addition to its political and social content, this story is loaded and coded with layers of meaning ready to unfold in our personal lives as well. Indeed this Manual for the Peacemaker presents us with the fact that if we are to change our world, we must first change ourselves. Thus the many experiential processes that follow each section of the story. Like Deganawidah we will discover our capacity to do the "impossible." We will find ways and means to stop feeding the toxic raiders of negative or self-diminishing thoughts; we will encounter the extraordinary ability that resides within each one of us for realizing the Mind of the Maker and the creative powers we each contain. We will seek our True Face, our true essence, and discover its guidance, as well as chopping down the tree of false opinion and attitudes which we still may hold. We will learn how to offer and receive condolence and nurturing. We will "comb away" those beliefs we have about ourselves that are no longer true and replace them with deep knowings which give us a larger life and a deeper truth. Finally, following a number of Native American practices, we will celebrate our journey with song and ritual, dance and dreaming, concluding it all with the planting of a Tree of Peace.

As we travel together through this great story, reliving its teachings, we hope to discover not only its revelatory power for our own lives and community, but what it has to say about the new confederacy of the planet that we're moving towards, a planetary society which honors the authenticity and the autonomy of each individual member, be it nation, state, tribe, or culture. The Iroquois Confederacy of Deganawidah and Hiawatha is thus a microcosm of this planetary society, with the great Tree of Peace that they planted as the grounding, the rooted basis for all nations to coexist in friendship and harmony and for all parts of ourselves to come together for new ways of being.

WHAT IS A MYSTERY SCHOOL?

If this process seems a mystery, it deserves to be so, for this volume is second in a series of books devoted to presenting material which grew out of our presentations in the Mystery School.

What is a Mystery School? It is my twentieth-century version of an ancient and honorable tradition going back millennia wherein men and women gathered to explore the mysteries of who we are, what we are here for, and what we may yet become. Once upon a time there were such schools in Egypt, Greece, Turkey, Persia, Afghanistan, India, China, Tibet, Ireland, England, France, Hawaii, the Americas, as well as in many places on the planet where the sacred called to the secular to illumine the mystery of existence.

The central questions of all Mystery Schools are: "How do we place the local self in service to the higher Self? How do we prepare to live a fuller life?" In our modern Mystery School, each session tries to answer these questions and to find ways to incorporate our discoveries into our lives. Thus we harvest what is available (or can be imagined) of the knowledge and traditions, rites and rituals of these ancient studies, imbuing them with new realities and discoveries. The weekends of the Mystery School are designed to provide rich experiences embracing sacred psychology, history of consciousness, music, theater, the world's cultures and peoples, philosophy, theology, poetry, high and low comedy, the new science, cosmology, metaphysics, and innovative ideas to provide a multifaceted, multilevel Time out of time.

Mystery School is both experiential and experimental. We stretch our bodies with psychophysical exercises, explore realms of psyche and spirit, create personal and community expressions of art and high play, and journey through dimensions of consciousness. Joined by a staff of eminent creative artists, we learn the movements, music, and dance as well as the arts of many ages and cultures. We participate in rituals, ceremonies, and high drama. We empower one another and embrace transformation. Virtually all of the exercises and processes involve restructuring of mental, physical, and psychological life to enable the activation of many of our extraordinary human potentials. Needless to say Mystery School is intellectually vigorous, psychologically challenging, and spiritually demanding. It requires a commitment to be open and available to the deep inner self. It is also frequently hilarious and zanily satiric. The work itself is mystifying, stimulating, depth-sourcing, soul-charging, and always celebrational.

The first three in this series of Mystery School books deals with material coming out of sessions on the mysteries of the Americas. In our work we have discovered that the history, culture, and landscapes of the Americas are coded with mysteries which, if explored, can yield perspectives on human possibilities that can literally reenchant the world. As voyagers into new continents of mind, body, and spirit, we can especially learn from the American experience of discovery ways to see familiar things from a deeper point of view. What is it about the Americas that has lured so many, for good or ill, to trek and meander, sail to and wander through, traverse endlessly back and forth in beauty and in shame, searching for a thousand different kinds of riches? For that matter, what is it that drives all of us to the "discovery" of new realms—physical, mental, emotional, and spiritual? To answer in Native American words, we seek the heart of the Great Mystery by learning to experience the truth of our personal Medicine, as well as our community and global Medicine.

In preparation for Mystery School each month, with the help of my associate Margaret Rubin, I essentially write a small book. This keeps us busy and constantly reading and studying! The transcript of each session is typed up by my much-valued colleague and friend Elisabeth Rothenberger, with each session running complete with lectures and experiential processes to well over 250 pages. To date there are about 100 such books of transcripts on my shelf, which are slowly but surely being rewritten, amplified, and published. This volume grew out of the Mystery School transcripts of 1992, extended through further study and our presentation of this seminar on five other occasions.

As these are edited and largely rewritten transcripts of the Mystery Schools, we have tried to retain the flavor of the sessions by keeping the colloquial use of speech as well as the odd turn of phrase in the lectures I gave and, most especially, in the exercises. Often the exercises are given spontaneously, created on the spot to fit the framework of the session. Thus the reader will note the cadence and curiosities of spoken speech, even when the exercises have been edited or rewritten.

This series of Mystery School books is for those of you who are committed to inner growth for yourselves so that you can join with others to generate a force strong enough to green the mind and body and soul of this planet. That is a major purpose of the Mystery School: revisioning the world and devoting ourselves to the task of sacred stewardship on behalf of our world. I created this school principally to help evolve a moral force for good in the world; I wanted to help engender a passion of purpose and deep commitment to live truly and beautifully in high service to others, whomever and whatever they may be. I can only hope that through this series the community of those who are in accord with these premises will bring some of the excitement, inspiration, and experience of the Mystery School to you who know as well that "These are the times, and we are the people."

NOTES

[1] Felix Cohen, "Americanizing the White Man," *American Scholar* 21: 2 (1952), p. 181.

[2] Ibid.

[3] This argument is an essential premise of Bruce E. Johansen's important work *Forgotten Founders: Benjamin Franklin, the Iroquois and the Rationale for the American Revolution* (Ipswich, Mass.: Gambit, Inc., 1982).

[4] Quoted in Donald A. Grinde, Jr., "Iroquois Political Theory and the Roots of American Democracy," in *Exiled in the Land of the Free*, Oren Lyons, John Mohawk, et al. (Santa Fe, N. Mex.: Clear Light Publishers, 1992), pp. 250–1.

I

EMBRACE THE OPEN MOMENT

The great story of Deganawidah begins, as all mythic tales begin, in mystery. The events and words spoken remind us of the prophecy in Isaiah, "and a virgin shall conceive and bear a child." In ancient times, it is said, a mother and daughter lived alone in a lodge among the Wendot people, later known as the Hurons, on the north shore of what is now called Lake Ontario. The actual place is said to be near the modern city of Kingston, Ontario. When the daughter became pregnant and declared to her mother that she had not known any man, her mother, perhaps like Joseph in another story, felt mortified at the stigma and humiliation that would come to them. Then, in a dream, an angelic presence, a courier from the Great Spirit Tarenyawagon, visited the mother and told her that the Holder of the Heavens and the Master of Life was sending a messenger, to be born of her virgin daughter, who would bring word of a New Peace and New Mind. The two women were charged to take good care of him, for he would be an incarnation of the Great Spirit sent to do his work on earth.

The mother sought to know more about the message her grandchild was to bring. She was told that his mission was to bring justice and new life in peace to all the people of the world. The women were warned that when Deganawidah had grown to manhood, he would one day announce that he was leaving his home to spread the New Mind among the nations. When this day came, they must not try to stop him.

Deganawidah's life began, thus, with the story found the world over of the one who comes from God as a Holy Child. He is born of a virgin, a woman made pregnant by extraordinary forces, and his mission is to change the nature of reality and bring a new possibility to people and their societies.

Why do the stories of many cultures tell us that the savior who is to make a difference is born of a virgin or conceived in ways that are wondrous strange? Perhaps these details are added after the fact to make sure we understand that this person is special. Or perhaps those individuals born to perform a radical task on behalf of the world must be free of ordinary patterning or of "normal" expectations and aspirations. It is a mystery. But any birth is a mystery, and every child deserves to be acknowledged as holy, a messenger from the Great Spirit, one who has come to perform a task for the good of humanity.

We can open further the mystery of the "immaculate conception" when we realize that immaculacy in many traditions describes extraordinary opportunity. Suddenly, all possibilities for new life are available. Old patterns, patrons, parentage are transcended; decadent and toxic ways are suspended; and the world and time are made new again. This pregnant moment is focused on the symbolic archetype of the "holy child," a being whose entry and passage into the world guides us through the gestation and labor pains of creating the possible human and the possible society.

After all, what is more potent than a child? Take all the world's treasures; put them on one side of a scale. Put a child, a newborn infant, on the other. Nothing will outweigh the glory, the potency, the richness of the child. Codings to last a million years are in its genes and chromosomes. Its being is celled of mysteries; its brain a star gate to a larger and more complex universe. A child is the God Force incarnate, and its potential is utterly open, completely available. Any child journeying from the darkness of the womb through the darkness of the earth offers his or her unique illumination to this world as part of the gift of life.

In the story of Deganawidah, then, we have an evolutionary agent who enters into time with a plan for a dynamic new order of peace. He has come to make straight the mind and the time. The name *Deganawidah* means The Master of Things. It also means, according to various Iroquois elders, He Who Thinks, Stone Mouth, or even The One with a Double Row of Teeth. The latter refers to the tradition that Deganawidah spoke with a stutter.

In many stories, the hero who incarnates to bring new vision to humanity either comes into the world with a handicap or soon acquires one. The handicap renders him or her vulnerable, perhaps exposed to ridicule. Adversity compels the hero to purify and clarify his or her message and spirit so that they may blaze forth brilliantly in spite of physical limitations. Thus Moses, who was also said to have a speech impediment, enlisted his brother Aaron to speak for him to Pharaoh, though he needed no interpreter to speak to Jehovah. Thomas Jefferson, who had a weak voice that would not carry to a crowd, became a writer of consummate skill to persuade others of his vision for authentic governance. The great educator and social activist Helen Keller, who was deaf, mute, and blind by the time she was nineteen months old, became an accomplished communicator, reaching millions through her books and lectures. We all know the story of one of the greatest physicists of our time, Stephen Hawking. Though his body is wasted by amyotrophic lateral sclerosis, his mind blazes forth to chart the inner workings of the universe.

After Deganawidah was born, some versions of the story tell us that his grandmother tried to drown him three times because of a prophecy that his life would not be favorable for his home tribe, the Hurons. (It can be said that this prediction came true. When the Hurons would not accept Deganawidah's message, he journeyed to other tribes. As the Iroquois Confederacy grew stronger, Huron war parties no longer won easy victories over the tribes of the confederacy and were ultimately defeated by them.)

Because of the prophecies, when the child was born, some say, his grandmother took him to the frozen lake, dug a circle in the ice and, with a heavy heart, placed him into the icy water. The next morning when Deganawidah's grandmother and mother woke up, they found the perfectly healthy baby lying between them. Twice more the grandmother tried to kill Deganawidah, and each time the baby was miraculously restored and found to be sleeping peacefully between the two women.

All over the world we find stories of the survival of the Holy Child in spite of fear, denial, even active hatred on the part of the older generations. This detail deserves to be noted. There is so much emphasis today on the woundings of childhood, which are indeed dreadful. Having reached epidemic proportions, such woundings do require acknowledgment and healing. Yet the great stories also tell us that holiness survives, that though we may be threatened and damaged by others, our essence can remain steadfast and strong.

From earliest childhood, then, Deganawidah was remarkable. He was honest, good, enormously intelligent, generous, and splendid looking. Animals loved him, and he seemed to enjoy rare powers of communication with them. He whistled to birds, and they came and sat on his shoulder. He conversed with fireflies in the night, and the morning saw him in communion with a bear. Rabbits came out of their burrows to be with him, and snakes swayed in front of him imparting their earthy wisdom. (In the Gnostic tales, Jesus is also described as being able to talk to the animals, much like his later follower Francis of Assisi.) The warlike Huron peoples found Deganawidah strange, and when he began to talk of peace, they saw him as foolish. War was where a young man and a tribe, too, found its identity; it was what made life worth living. War expeditions against the neighboring tribes, especially the Huron's distant cousins, the Mohawks, who lived south of Lake Ontario, were a fact of life. While the young Huron boys and adolescents practiced the arts of war, Deganawidah thought and reflected, making plans for a new idea of peace.

As Deganawidah grew out of adolescence, he not only continued to talk of a new society based on peace and friendship, but he frequently offered advice to others on improving their lives and on the governing of the tribe. Coming as it did from a teenager without office or authority, Deganawidah's counsel was not appreciated. He also declared to all who would listen that his message had been inspired directly by the Great Spirit and that he himself was the prophet of the Master of Life. As you can imagine, people responded in much the same way that we might upon hearing a similar claim—with scorn. It was Jesus of Nazareth who once remarked ruefully, "A prophet is not without honor except in his own country," and Deganawidah was no exception to this ancient rule. On a more secular level, it is a truism that no man is a hero to his valet, or to his secretary. For those of us with neither valets nor secretaries, our closest friends keep us humble. But in the face of a radical task, such as that of creating a possible society, Deganawidah teaches us that we may need to go out into the world, away from those who watched us grow up and who think they know us best. It is a sad fact that these are the ones who will not believe us, because they see us in a limited way. Thus we must travel elsewhere to spread our message. The lesson here is that we should never allow the disparagement of friends to dissuade us from our true mission.

The taunting continued: How dare Deganawidah say he was the Prophet of God! Why not just leave, Deganawidah, and go bother some other people with this ridiculous message? So Deganawidah left the settlement and wandered deep into the forest seeking clarity and spiritual insight. As is the way of such quests, we can imagine that he fasted and prayed, allowing himself only an occasional sip of water and focusing his attention on what he should do and where he should go.

"Great Spirit," he prayed over and over again, "show me what it is that you wish me to do among the nations. Show me the plan of my mission."

After many days, his mind open and altered by fasting and prayer, a vision came to him. He saw clearly the prodigious work he was to do in the world, the work of going from person to person and from tribe to tribe persuading them to take up the ways of peace and the New Mind. The *kairos*, the loaded time, was upon him. Returning to his mother and grandmother, he addressed them with great affection, saying, "The time has come for me to set out on my mission in the world. I shall now build my canoe. Know that far away on many lakes and rivers I go seeking the council smoke of nations, holding my course toward the sunrise. It is my business to stop the shedding of blood among human beings."[1] It is as if Deganawidah was saying, as Jesus had, "I must be about my Father's business." With their similar details and words, the stories of Deganawidah and Jesus seem to come to us from the collective unconscious, bringing us great patterns—manuals, almost—of how the work of world-changing is to be accomplished.

On the day of his departure, his grandmother and mother accompanied Deganawidah as he dragged the white canoe he had made toward the banks of the Great Beautiful Lake. It is here that we learn in the stories that the canoe was carved out of stone. As he prepared to push his strange craft into the water, he told his grandmother and mother not to look for his return. Nevertheless, according to the story, he provided a way for them to learn of his success or failure. He pointed to a lone tree standing on a hilltop and told them that they could make a small cut in the tree when they wished to learn how he was. If blood poured from the gash, they would know that he was dead and his mission a failure; but if there was no blood, they could be assured that he was well and that his work was succeeding.

The message-giving capacities of trees is one of the gifts that many earth-wise people know. In the circle of life all things are present and connected, and trees seem to have the ability to know of, and to mourn, the destructive side of humanity. Trees, as we shall see, are a major part of Deganawidah's story and his mission. An implicit message of his story is that not only are trees vital to the life force of the planet, but also specific trees may share some essential part of each individual's life force.

As Deganawidah's mother and grandmother said farewell, they remarked on the unique, impossible character of the canoe. "You have made your canoe out of stone," his grandmother said sadly. "It will certainly sink. You cannot set out on a journey in a stone canoe. What you plan to do in talking about peace is impossible. You must be as crazy as everybody says."

Deganawidah replied, "No, it will float. You will see. And by this impossible action, you shall know that my words are true, and that I shall bring peace to the nations."

With that, he pushed the canoe into the water and paddled away! His mother and grandmother were astonished.

Why a stone canoe? Stone is the most compacted form of earth, yet formed of star stuff, with a sense of eternity about it. By grounding himself thoroughly in a stone canoe, Deganawidah connected himself to earth and its indestructibility. Moreover, setting out in a stone canoe, knowing that he could not only keep it from sinking but also travel in it to new lands, he knew himself capable of performing the impossible. He could do so, he said, because his words were true; to the Native American, we must remember, truth has both overwhelming power and a quality of bedrock. Thus setting out on a mission across a great lake in a stone canoe represents both the willingness to undertake an impossible task and an awareness of the power and authority of a truth such as the one Deganawidah carried, that endless warmaking is a crime against life. As we shall see, paddling a stone canoe became a metaphor for many of Deganawidah's tasks, and the actual work of doing so was only the first of his difficulties.

When we think of the seemingly impossible things that people have done, we find that pushing the boundaries of the possible is natural for the human race. In fact, it comes with the human condition and is what makes life worth living. Attempting the impossible hones our pluck and cunning and calls up resources that we never knew we had. The poet Rainer Maria Rilke's words on this subject are most apt: "We must assume our existence as broadly as we in any way can; everything, even the unheard of, must be possible in it. This is at bottom the only courage that is demanded of us: to have courage for the most strange, the most inexplicable."

We are all familiar with acts of daring and invention that illumine the history of human endeavor. The discovery and exploration of the antipodes of the earth, or finding a cure to a fatal disease against all odds, the creation of the United Nations, the linking of the earth's peoples through electronics, the conquest of hundreds of years of prejudice: these indeed seem impossible on a gigantic scale. But when we look at individual cultures, we startle at the vision of ordinary people daily everywhere doing things which seem extraordinary. One thinks of the Inuit (Eskimo) people, guided only by the odors of wind and snow, finding their way to their homes through a shifting, blinding white landscape. At the other end of the earth, I recall seeing in southern India Kathakali dancers simultaneously move their cheeks, foreheads, ear and eye muscles, while making intricate and varied gestures with each of their ten fingers and moving the muscles of their abdomens in impossible ways and dancing the complex steps in concert with the other dancers. Then in northern India a week later, I saw and tested yogis as they sat in subfreezing temperatures in the Himalayas, wearing only loincloths and generating so much body heat that they were able to dry wet sheets that were placed on their bare shoulders. Here at home, working with altered states of consciousness, I have elicited from musically trained research subjects entire symphonic compositions in five minutes of clock time, compositions that then took many weeks to write down and an hour to perform. I have seen seminar participants descend into previously impossible reaches of their minds where they have discovered remarkable works of poetry, novels, dissertations, and creative discoveries which they have been able to bring back into ordinary space and time.

From all this and more I have come to the conclusion that given opportunity and motivation, given the passion for achieving a goal, a discovery, a way of being, a redressing of wrongs, people will do the impossible, either by themselves or in concert with others. My old friend, anthropologist and world grandmother Margaret Mead, regularly took on impossible tasks and showed us how it was done. "Never doubt that a small group of thoughtful committed citizens can change the world," she said. "Indeed, it is the only thing that ever has."

NOTE

---

[1] Many of the more stately and liturgical statements Deganawidah makes throughout the book are taken from *The White Roots of Peace*, by Paul A. Wallace.

PADDLING THE STONE CANOE/ DOING THE IMPOSSIBLE

TIME: One hour.

MATERIALS: Writing materials.

MUSIC: Environmental sounds: waves on a beach.

INSTRUCTIONS FOR GOING SOLO: Put the instructions for the Guide on tape. You can also add if you wish, as background, the sounds of waves lapping on a beach. Be careful to allow yourself enough time and sufficient pauses to get the full benefit of the processes.

This three-part process offers you the opportunity to be charged with the spirit of the Peacemaker as well as discovering something about your capacity to do the "impossible."

In Part One you will discover and write in poetry or prose your ideas and feelings about the nature and practice of peace. In Part Two you will be guided in a meditation to a state of receptivity in which you receive the quality of the Peacemaker. Finally, in Part Three, you will emulate Deganawidah by paddling your own stone canoe while recalling the "impossible" tasks that you have already accomplished and then, still paddling, anticipate those "impossible" things you have yet to accomplish as you continue on life's journey.

Now, we all know it as our job in this open moment of the planet's history to bring peace—peace that is so rich and full of flavor that it makes sense to make peace. Once, on a late night National Public Radio program, I said that peace should be sexy. Several days later, Clifford Browder, an elderly poet who had listened to the show, sent me the following poem inspired by my remarks:

Peace is not
Sterile gauze, a snowflake, an insipid dove
It's feisty and rich

Don't let the war boys hog it all
The spit, the spice and the glamour.

Peace is potency
Reaching and sprouting
Budding and branching

It's lifting things
A good scrap
A hot wrestle and a cool scrub
Cleansing and hope.

Peace is the empowerment of dust
Whispers of the song before origin
As out of seed
The cathedral of the body builds itself

It's spasms and metamorphoses
The vertigo
Of mind dancing
With the fecundator
To the music of need.

Peace
Is little orange bees
Spotted ladybugs on white campions
Late June with a stink of linden
Prickles and burrs

It's wild grapes in a bramble
A tough nut

Lovers churning
Through the night, at noon, in the morning
A juicy comeuppance
For the grim suppressors.

Peace
Is for the star-biters and the rooted
Don't be dainty
Go at it
Hammer and tong.

Peace is not purity
Limp, neat and dry.
It's sexy.

It is a dynamic, green-growing, sap-rising concept, this peacemaking and, when it works, it renews both individuals and communities. It moves beyond the brass bands and parades, the costumed glamour, the decorations and declarations which we have used for millennia to ignite the fires of war. We become Peacemakers by holding the peace force in our hearts so fully that our very being exudes peace and courage. We become Peacemakers by living in a state of consciousness that invites sharing and cooperation, healing and mutual growth. We become Peacemakers by knowing the ebullience in the bones that comes of the goodly and gracious life.

SCRIPT FOR THE GUIDE:

PART ONE

We will begin by listening to the poem "Peace" by Clifford Browder and then write our own version in poetry or prose of the many forms of peace. (The Guide reads the poem and then says:) Now begin your own version, starting perhaps with the words, "Peace is . . ."

or even "Peace is not . . ." As you write, allow your mind and feelings about peace to roam the ramparts of all possibilities, including curious connections, fertile and fascinating metaphors. Don't stint; let your mind be open to peace streamings from every direction, finding linkages to peace and peacemaking especially in places you never looked before. You will have ten minutes of clock time, equal subjectively to all the time you need, to write your piece on peace. And now begin. (Ten minutes, or less if the participants seem to have finished early.)

(The Guide will then have the participants read to each other and to the group what they have written.)

PART TWO

I ask you now to sit up in a comfortable position and close your eyes. Begin to stretch, arms first up so that the spine pulls up, then arms back so that you open your chest, feeling an expansion in the heart area. Just stretch and open, open and stretch. Would you also thump gently on your thymus at the middle of your chest above the heart area, which is, by the way, wonderful for reminding your immune system that you are grateful for its existence.

Let us begin by invoking the spirit of Deganawidah and Hiawatha as archetypes of peacemaking, persuaders and teachers of the way of peace. A legend tells that before he left his people, Deganawidah promised that if they needed a renewal of peace, they had only to speak his name and he would return to teach them again. The ancient peoples knew that there is power in a name, so our invocation may simply be the name by which Deganawidah is known—Peacemaker. (Members of the Iroquois nation hold the name Deganawidah as so sacred that they speak it aloud only in ceremony; otherwise they call him Peacemaker, Prophet, or The Man from the North.) Repeat, if you wish, the preferred name with me now: *Peacemaker. Peacemaker. Peacemaker. Peacemaker.*

If you are moved to do so, your invocation may also include words of peace that reflect the message and spirit of Deganawidah, or you may find yourself speaking messages of peace that are appropriate to today's world but which come from the same creative Source that sourced the Peacemaker. (One minute.)

Now, I invite you to imagine or sense that you are standing on the shore of a large lake with your feet in the water. Behind you is a thick forest filled with trees—maple, chestnut, oak, elm, and pine. You can see, far out in the middle of a lake, an Indian man paddling a white canoe carved out of stone. Impossible as it seems, it glides gracefully through the waters. The man is paddling toward you. Each dip of his paddle sends ripples moving out, which become part of the lake's waves gently advancing toward you. They are waves of peace and of the knowledge of peace. They are waves that carry vibrations from the Mind of the Maker, the Heart of Life. They are waves holding the potency of peace and the creation of peace in our lives, in our communities, in our world.

Information born on these waves may not reveal itself to you all at once, but it is moving toward you, reaching out to you as you stand on the shore with your feet in the gently lapping waters. Waves of new possibility, waves of peacefulness. Waves that enliven you with new energies, ideas for helping to bring about a better world. And you feel yourself not just washed by these waves, but refreshed, renewed, made open and vulnerable to a whole new possibility. And everything that you are, your entire life experience, rises to meet the peace waves, mingling now to bring a new richness and depth of understanding to the meaning and purpose of your life.

The waves are coming faster now, as the man in the canoe comes closer and closer to you as you stand on the shore. And as the canoe reaches the shore where you are, allow the tip of the canoe to reach up and touch your heart, creating there a great lake, a Lake of Peace. Now the Peacemaker paddles his white canoe into the lake of your heart, which itself grows wider and wider until it touches the horizon. And as this happens, the waves in the lake of your heart meet and join with the waves of the Great Lake which carries the canoe of the Peacemaker. And you allow Deganawidah, Peacemaker, to enter fully into the lake of your heart, granting you something of the New Mind, new heart, new understanding of the message, the challenge, and the task of peacemaking . . .

And the peace moves in you, and it is you. And you know yourself as Peacemaker. And you say in your heart, and you say aloud the words that recur throughout this great story when peace is received: *I take hold of it. I embrace it. I take hold of it. I embrace it. I take hold of it. I embrace it. I take hold of it. I embrace it.*

Holding this peace as a precious gift, we enter the next part of the story, recalling our own impossible journeys in the equivalent of a stone canoe. For it is by regularly doing those things which the world considers impossible, that we find the courage and momentum to bring new possibilities into time.

PART THREE

Please find yourself a partner. Then holding the Peacemaker in your heart, would you now physically emulate climbing into a canoe with your partner. The canoe is on the shore of the Great Lake of your heart. Actually assume the position of sitting or kneeling in the canoe, with both of you holding a paddle, one in front, one behind, sitting close enough so that you can hear each other's words. Feel the canoe push out into the lake. Now begin to paddle energetically with your imaginary paddle. As you paddle, look along the shore for scenes or memories of times when you did the impossible. Remember that Deganawidah's ability to float a stone canoe is a signal that his words are true. So look for or sense a time or a place when your truth shone so bravely that you were able to do impossible things. As you remember these things, tell your canoeing partner about them.

Here is an example of how this part of the process works, drawn from the demonstration given by Jean Houston and her associate Peggy Rubin at the Mystery School:

Jean: I see myself there on the shore as a child who hated to write. And there I am as an adolescent, and there I am in college, and even through graduate school, still hating to write. In fact, with few exceptions, I still dislike writing. There is nothing I like less to do, and nothing for which I feel less talent. People ask me if I "channel" my books, and I tell them, "I fight for every word!" And yet I have produced, to date, fifteen published books, and I continue to write a small book every month for Mystery School as well as work on my other seminars. I see now that I decided to embrace the impossible and just get on with it and do it. Why? Because my message demanded expression in written words and my inner truth urged me to keep paddling, keep writing, until I moved beyond the blocks in my mind.

I can also see myself as inspired by whatever is the Peacemaker in me and by that sense of my higher task in this world. For I know I've got to put this work of developing the possible human out there in writing so that other people can use it. So despite the fact that I'd much rather just give lectures and invent and conduct processes, I end up writing. Given my considerable distaste for writing, I think I am doing the impossible. And you, Peggy?

Peggy: On the shore of the lake of my heart, I see a little girl on a farm in south Texas, lying on the roof of a barn and dreaming up into the night sky of stars—a fierce little warrior Christian soldier child who wanted to change everybody into a believer in the Methodist God. Further along the shore I see the incredulous young woman realizing not only that great numbers of people did not believe in the Methodist God, but that they did not harbor in their heart of hearts any desire ever to believe in my God. Still further I see the young woman beginning the progress of learning to see how others saw, even to practice belief in what others believe.

Finally I watch her foot fall on the earth having read that once there was a time when women walked safe and knew a feminine presence in the realm of God, and her foot remembers that time. Literally the earth and all the heavens opened to her, and she began the practice of seeing the infinite roads and footpaths and rivers to the Source and the equally diverse and thrilling pathways that the Source takes to find the human heart. So there are two impossibles here: one that that little girl should ever be able to see what I now see, and two, that I should ever have been that little girl. Yet, I also *see the truth within me of the love that breathes through it all and was always a truth within me.*

Begin now to talk back and forth, telling each other about the things that you accomplished even though they seemed impossible. You may find it easier to close your eyes and open your inner sensing so that these things reveal themselves as scenes along the shore of this Great Lake. Describe them for your partner. But keep the active paddling going, moving the body forward and back as you paddle. (Five to ten minutes.)

Now becoming quiet, stop, and just let the waves of peace move through you. Feel the codings, the wave patterns of the Peacemaker as part of your being. Whether this feeling rises to consciousness as words or as images does not matter. It is that patterning, that pulse of reenchantment that is now your rightful portion. As it moves within you, it informs your awareness of what you are here to do in this world. So now begin to paddle again and to speak of what may seem impossible that still needs to be done. Even though the world, or your friends, or even you yourself feel it to be impossible, you are going to do it.

Here is another example from the Mystery School session:

Jean: I am being asked to do the impossible, and I have to find ways of doing it in a fashion that honors while it informs. I'm being called upon to advise governments, bioregions, cultures, on the creative and dynamic recreation of their social forms, on how to pattern their education, their health, their welfare in such a way that they can keep the autonomy, the genius of their culture, while they also begin to become planetary citizens, member cultures of the emerging planetary civilization. And I need to do this in such a way that I still have time for reflection, for my own deepening, and for not becoming ill in Third World countries, since I'm in and out of them all the time, and my American body is accustomed to American germs and water and food.

So my impossible task is keeping the proper balance between personal health and deepening and this impossible task that I have accepted in the world. And I also have to make a living so that I can support the impossible task of being a global midwife which is largely done for free.

Peggy: The thing that I want to do that feels impossible at the moment is to let go of the enormous pleasure I get in anger, in war thoughts. When I went to see the play Ms. Saigon *recently, I was moved beyond the possibility of being moved because of the sadness and the terror and the mistake and the pain of war. So the things that touch me the most deeply are the results of war. And I need to see if there's a way, which feels at the moment impossible, to turn that utterly around, so that my rich, wild, joyous, and sometimes deeply sad life is removed from the need for war inside myself and with other people. Or the need to do righteous battle, or unrighteous battle, which is endemic in my nature. And that feels impossible to me. I'd rather float a stone canoe any day.*

Now begin to paddle again, speaking back and forth to each other about that which may be deemed impossible, yet calls to you so deeply you know that somehow you're going to do it. Remember that it's only a small part of you that thinks that a thing is impossible. There are other parts that are utterly innocent of the odds and don't know that it's impossible at all. The older part of your brain—the old survivor reptilian brain that protects you—may keep warning, "Hey, no way! Don't do that. It's something new. It's not safe. Forget it." But the curious, innocent, inventive, newer part of your brain in the cerebral cortex says, "What's next? Let's try that and see what happens." So parts of you will continue to think that things are impossible, but other parts will give you both the impetus to keep crossing thresholds and the power to begin to cocreate with time and history in this impossible, wonderful time in which we live.

Sometimes when Deganawidah nears the shore where he must accomplish even more impossible things, a great wind comes up to stop him. That's when he puts in extra energy and oomph. Holding on to the vision and the details of that impossible thing that you have yet to achieve, put more strength into your paddling, more vigorous and vivid life into the image you are holding, and you will bring yourself closer to the shore where your task will be realized. Allies, qualities of courage and endurance, as well as skills you didn't know you had, will all come to your aid there, saying: "Blessed are the innocent who take on impossible things that need doing, for they are the ones who get to the shore." Begin paddling now and telling each other about the impossible things you have yet to do. (Ten minutes.)

(After the time allotted, the Guide will bring the process to a close by suggesting that the participants write or draw in their journals what they have discovered about the impossible things they have done and have yet to do. Suggest that each person select one of the impossible tasks they have yet to do and spend a few moments with their partners deciding how to take the first step toward achieving that impossible accomplishment, asking themselves, "What can be done today?" The partners are invited to acknowledge their belief that the things to be done shall be done with words like those used in this story, "I embrace your ideas and see their results rippling through the world; your plans are now a part of my life and my being; I thank you for daring to do the impossible. Our stone canoe will float and keep floating!")

2

DEGANAWIDAH
IN THE WORLD

▲▲▲

Deganawidah paddled south on Lake Ontario (*Sganyadaii-yo*, The Beautiful Great Lake) toward the far shore in what is now northern New York state, the land of the tribes that he would consolidate as the Five Nations of the Iroquois Confederacy. As he approached the shore, he saw men running along the beach toward him, drawn by the appearance of his white stone canoe. We can imagine their sense of wonder as they realized what they were seeing: "Paddling a stone canoe! How can this be, this wonder, this impossible thing? What can it mean? Who might this person be?" They rushed to the water, urging him to come closer so that they could question him.

We can also imagine Deganawidah's feelings. This was the first moment of his great mission, and these men his first contacts. He asked the men who they were. They told him they were hunters who had left their hill settlements.

Deganawidah looked around and saw that there were no fields of corn, no signs of permanent dwellings. "Does anyone live here?" he asked.

"No," they replied.

"Then why have you come here, where there is nothing for you, not even a single human settlement?"

"Because it's too dangerous to live anywhere anymore," the men answered. "We have had to leave even our hill settlements because of the incessant wars that plague us."

The hunters then told Deganawidah a terrible story of unending intertribal warfare—of destruction, starvation, and death; of feuding factions, lawlessness, constant incitement to war, slaughter of innocent women and children, even cannibalism. Headhunters were rife in the land. Human life had deteriorated so that even deaths from accident, disease, or old age were thought to be caused by black magic. A soothsayer would tell the family of someone who had died who was responsible for the magical act that had caused the death and where to find them, either within the tribe or in another tribe. The family of the dead person then set about exacting vengeance and retribution, which resulted in a ceaseless cycle of suspicion, rage, and killing. The eastern woodlands were stalked by assassins, anarchy reigned, and people lived in constant fear of reprisal. Fear breeds weakness, for in this state there is little time or energy for developing other areas of life. Out of weakness, men too often turn to more war to assert what little power remains to them.

Recent years have shown how mindlessly cruel are societies who live in constant dread of each other. From Beirut to Belfast to Bosnia we witness a sickness of soul that breeds a constant chronicle of unspeakable horrors. The psychological and spiritual fallout that comes from living in such conditions deadens the mind while it savages the heart. The twentieth century, perhaps the cruelest and most inexplicable of all centuries, has created shock waves in the psyche that threaten to numb what remains of our resources for turning the world around. The cruelties of nations and the violence of individuals are our media's daily meat, a fact that adds to the hopeless despair which causes many to turn towards the ideological fortresses of fundamentalism and simplistic solutions.

As for Deganawidah, here was his opportunity; this was the place to begin. Stuttering, with a voice that legend tells us was harsh and unpleasing, he told the hunters to go back to their village and tell their chief that "the G-g-g-good N-n-news of the G-g-great P-p-peace has c-c-come."

"Really?" the hunters replied in amazement both at the message and its delivery.

"Y-y-yes," Deganawidah replied. "And your v-village is g-going to be free of t-troubles. The Great Creator, f-from whom we are all d-d-escended, sent me to establish the G-Great P-peace among you."

"Yes, all right, we'll tell him," the hunters said as they began to edge away from the shore.

But Deganawidah called them back. "W-wait. D-don't go. I've g-got m-more to t-tell you." He then told them that they would no longer kill one another. Nations would cease warring upon each other. If their chief asked from whence this peace would come, they should tell him, "The messenger of good tidings of peace and power will arrive in a few days."

This part of the story is similar to Native legends from other parts of the country which speak of a sacred messenger who appears first to hunters who are asked to tell their people to prepare for his or her arrival. The best known is the story of White Buffalo Woman of the Lakota people of the Great Plains. She, too, arrived in a time of terrible strife and starvation, appearing first to hunters and sending them back to their homes with the news that she was coming. When she came to the village and was welcomed, she gave the people many of their ceremonies, including the ritual of making and smoking the pipe as a form of communion with all living things and with the Great Spirit. She also provided the buffalo for food and its hide for shelter and clothing. White Buffalo Woman arrived at the time of the greatest need, when the tribes of the Plains were decimated by hunger.

Perhaps the troubles in the eastern woodlands which inspired the coming of Deganawidah were also caused by hunger. Throughout the story, Deganawidah emphasized the importance of good diet and agriculture, especially by recognizing the deer as a gift from the Creator, providing both a source of food and a symbol of the need to work together to maintain strength. Certainly the Iroquois had so weakened themselves that they were prey to other warring tribes, especially the Hurons who attacked them from the north and the Mohicans, from the east.

The terrors that assaulted the Iroquois at this time are the ones that play so vivid a role in our lives today: that all-too-human search for revenge for wrongs done to us or imagined by us. But as we shall see, the story of Deganawidah shows us that it is possible to end this vengeance cycle. This is one of his most potent teachings and, if it could be applied today, we would all be on the road to a very different society,

Before they returned to their hill settlements, the amazed hunters asked the stranger his name. Deganawidah, it is said, replied without stuttering: "I come from the West. I go toward the sunrise. I am called Deganawidah in the World."

Notice that Deganawidah did not say, "I am called Deganawidah by the world." Rather, he said that his whole name was Deganawidah in the World. This phrasing suggests that Deganawidah knew that he was living as an agent of an archetypal power, that he was the outward manifestation, the living incarnate form in space and time of an inward spiritual power. It is as if he had said, "I am Deganawidah, the One Who Knows How To Make Things Work in the World, a representative on earth of the Mind of the Maker." In this he bears some resemblance to Jesus, who said, "I and my Father are one." Also like Jesus, Deganawidah was in a state of communion and dynamic connection with the archetypal realm of spirit. Throughout history, certain individuals have felt a similar identification with spirit, manifesting as archetypes of divine or sacred persons or qualities. This is especially so at times when the world needs to change and grow, when new ways of being and thinking and doing are necessary if the human species is to take its next steps. Then it seems that certain men and women are inspired by the particular spiritual or archetypal presences that contain the evolutionary information needed to guide the next stage of human development. By tapping into an energy that is larger than their local life, such individuals are energized to engage in extraordinary activities and to deliver inspired teachings.

The world of the Iroquois at this time was desperately in need of a new dispensation, one that would restore peace and bring in a new model of social behavior and governance to ensure and develop this peace. The archetype most needed was that of the Peacemaker. Deganawidah became its agent, bringing a higher knowledge and practice of peace into the world. He was a bridge from the Mind of the Maker, that domain of spirit wherein all the great evolutionary patterns are held. Because he carried the energy and knowledge of the Peacemaker, even those whose lives had been given over to war and violence were transformed by his presence and his message.

In today's world there is a need for this communion with the Mind of the Maker to be experienced democratically; more of us need to recognize and welcome our sourcing in the Great Spirit. We are all agents of the evolutionary process. Without grandiosity or inflation, we need to be willing to clarify our sense of being part of a Larger Family whose origins are in the depth dimensions. Then we can both experience and testify to the message we carry from these dimensions.

In addition, we must learn to listen to the God-in-hiding in others, as many indigenous people are able to do. Like the hunters, we can come to ask humbly of others, "Who are you really, and what is your message?" And when we ourselves are asked that question, we need to respond truthfully and courageously as Deganawidah does. Notice that he is willing to speak his truth to anyone who will listen, but he does not demand or threaten. Rather, he persuades and encourages others to share his vision. Would it not be wonderful to be able to answer a question about our identity and our purpose with the deepest knowing of the soul? To do so is to realize that we are a particular focalization in space and time of the God-Self and to become more and more accustomed to being sourced from this Self. From this knowing, we can work in the world of space and time as well as in the archetypal world that underlies this one, attending to the glory of the unfolding creation that yearns to enter into time. Then perhaps, we can say with Deganawidah, with Thoreau, with Gandhi, and with Martin Luther King, "I am part of the Mind of the Maker. My message is that there is strength in nonviolence, and I know of ways to show you what I mean."

In his wonderful book on the psychology of war and peace *Out of Weakness*, Andrew Bard Schmookler says, "The task of making peace . . . is not just a matter of realpolitik; it is a matter also of spirit. It requires us not only to deal with the practicalities of our place in the mundane world, but to confront our place in the cosmic order of things. We must know who we are and what we are doing— know not only with the intellect but with our whole being, in the way that mystics have always achieved the knowledge that has given our species its deepest guidance."[1]

The work of making peace begins with the task of making ourselves whole. But wholeness may well require that we consciously join the larger reality of which we are a part, that we consciously agree to become some aspect of the Mind of the Maker in the World. I have written in other books of the knowledge and inspiration that can be opened in our lives when we embrace those primary constellations of energy known as archetypes, especially when we activate within ourselves those forces that seem to be most needed in our time, such as the Peacemaker. This task is both delicate and profound, for it requires rigorous human homework and the willingness to pare away one's unskilled behaviors, becoming more and more attuned to "being love" or "being peace" without any sense of superiority or what Buddhists call attachment.

In just this way, Deganawidah's connection with the archetype of the Peacemaker was so charged with power that the hunters felt it instantly. They hurried to their village and told everyone about the impressive visitor and his message of peace. The telling awakened hope among the people and their chiefs who realized for the first time that peace was possible. Even hearing the words that a messenger of peace was coming fired their imaginations and opened the doors of their minds and hearts to the joy of such a prospect.

Perhaps that is a necessary first step to our becoming authentic peacemakers: announce to the desperate, hungry hunters within that the Peacemaker is coming, have them carry the word to all parts of the mind-body system that warfare is outmoded and new possibilities are at hand. The most ancient part of the brain, the reptilian complex at the back of the skull given over to protection and survival, will undoubtedly be cautious. But the newer parts of the brain, the emotional limbic system and the neocortex, will, perhaps, hope and wonder. Speak words of power and metaphor to them, simple and memorable. What could be better than the words that Deganawidah used: "I am part of the Mind of the Maker. I bring the promise of peace and clear ways to achieve it. I leave the old ways and go towards the sunrise." If we can persuade the ancient adversaries within to listen to the possibility of peace, we are already halfway to making true peace in whatever we do.

Meanwhile, as news of Deganawidah's imminent arrival spread through the settlement, he himself made his way deeper into the forest, seeking other individuals who could help prove the effectiveness of his message. He stopped first at the home of a lone woman of the Erie nation. Her lodge, located on the warrior path running between east and west, was a neutral resting place. Warriors of every tribe could stop there, leave their weapons at the door, and be fed and refreshed. As was her custom, the woman welcomed the stranger. She was surprised to learn that he was not a warrior, and when Deganawidah spoke to her of his intention to end the fighting among the tribes who used the path which ran beside her door, the woman was shocked. She, too, had lived perpetually in war and dread, knowing no other possibility, and so she questioned the feasibility of such a thing. The stories tell us that this was the first time Deganawidah spoke in depth about the nature of the peace he was to bring and about the changes in mind and behavior needed to bring it about. He challenged the woman to be the first to reform her style of living and working. "Please don't serve the warriors, the raiders, the destroyers anymore," he told her. "The Great Peace will be served if you no longer feed the raiders."

"But that's what I do," the woman protested. "That's my work. That's who I am. I am the woman who feeds the warriors."

"Serve a higher cause," Deganawidah admonished her, "the cause of peace. Don't nourish the raiders. Then you will discover who you really are."

Here again Deganawidah made a radical request, an extraordinary announcement, and offered information that provided a practical course of action to begin the process of becoming peace. For us the question resounds: Who are the raiders, anyway? On the simplest psychological level, the raiders may be seen as toxic thoughts and conditions we dwell upon, those negative self-judgments or patterns of behavior that we turn into habits that order our lives. We welcome such patterns, set up housekeeping with them, give them nourishment, because such thoughts have a real tang for us. In other periods of our lives, we turn away from them for a time, but suddenly they rise again, poisonous tokens from the past reborn into our lives, often bringing with them similar circumstances and relationships. And we think, I haven't had that one in twenty years! But with the return of the old way of being comes that familiar bittersweet, poignant anguish. Then, if we are not careful, we become sentimental, welcoming our raiders like old friends and starting again to feed them. This is why they have come. They plead for our attention, reminding us of the years we have spent with them, appealing to our long history together. We are still part of you, they insist. And as it was with the Erie woman who fed the warriors traveling the path beside her door, the raiders assure us that taking care of them is what we are supposed to do.

On the social level Deganawidah's request to the woman was also extraordinary. He asked her to give up her livelihood or, at the very least, to change its source substantially. An inference to be drawn from this is that in order to be peacemakers in society, we must be willing to look at everything we do with new eyes and, if need be, to make radical alterations in our careers and professions. Are we engaged in what the Buddha termed right livelihood, or do we promote products or activities that contribute to the toxic environment? And if our work is socially responsible, do we treat it as something that we do automatically, caring little for improving its premises or enhancing its methods and designs? Do we regard it as "just a job," thus serving the toxic raiders within the profession who feed from the table of our own indifference? Instead, Deganawidah challenges us, we must inspect with a cool eye to observe exactly how our actions and our attitudes affect life around and within us, and then begin to live with greater awareness and more simplicity. We cannot embrace the New Mind by just sitting around and talking about it. It demands that we alter not just our thinking, but our way of living down to the smallest details.

NOTE

[1] Andrew Bard Schmookler, *Out of Weakness: Healing the Wounds That Drive Us to War* (New York: Bantam, 1988), p. 29.

STOP FEEDING THE TOXIC RAIDERS

TIME: Two hours or more.

MATERIALS: A large empty room or, preferably, an outdoor space where participants can make an unholy mess. Each participant will need at least three big sheets of newsprint or other paper as well as drawing materials. Each should bring a selection of soft messy foods, like jello, jellies, peanut butter, margarine, marshmallows, cooked oatmeal, canned chili, applesauce, pureed vegetables, etc. They should wear bathing suits or old clothes and have soap, shampoo, and towels standing by. If Part Two is to be done indoors because of the weather, the floor should be covered with painter's drop cloths. For Part Three, tape large pieces of paper together to make one very large piece of paper on which all the participants can draw a huge plan for higher consciousness. The participants should also bring wonderful tasty foods to share in a concluding feast and celebration at the end of the process.

MUSIC: Native American drumming.

INSTRUCTIONS FOR GOING SOLO: This process really needs to be done with at least one other person. Put the Guide's instructions on tape and be sure to have a concluding feast with your friend. If you absolutely must go solo, then follow the instructions, but when it comes to the food fight, use a large mirror to hurl the sloppy food against.

SCRIPT FOR THE GUIDE:
In this process we become vividly aware of our own toxic raiders and destroyers. When we fall into the habit of investing time and

emotional energy in feeding our toxic thoughts, we enter a chronic state of debilitating negativity. In other words, we make war on ourselves. This state can become so automatic that we may forget what healthy thought—what both the Buddhists and Deganawidah refer to as *right mindfulness*—is like. We play the same harsh notes over and over again on the keyboard of our consciousness, even when the events or circumstances that provoked these negative feelings are long gone or reconciled.

(At this point, the Guide may wish to invite the participants to share and discuss this problem as it occurs in their lives.)

How, then, do we go about breaking these deep-seated patterns? How do we stop feeding the toxic raiders, as Deganawidah asks us to do?

Part One

The first step is discovering what your raiders look like. Take out your drawing materials and place at least three of the large sheets in front of you. Begin to draw quickly on each of the sheets a cartoon of one of the recurrent raiders of your mind and being that you continue to feed. Draw what these recurrent raiders look like to you, whether they be toxic thoughts, or qualities, or moods, or even recurrent types of relationships or people whom you continue to nourish. These raiders are such a familiar and expected a part of your life that even if they have been gone for some time, when they suddenly reappear, you prepare food for them and nourish them by the attention you give them.

Draw these cartoons quickly. Try not to name the raiders first; words keep us from seeing the full power and irony of who and what they are. (Drumming plays while the drawing goes on. Ten to fifteen minutes.)

(The Guide should observe the process and be flexible about the time, ending the process when the participants seem finished. Then the Guide should invite sharing about what the participants have discovered.)

In the Mystery School version, here is what two participants said:

Woman Participant: I have three that I could think of right away. This first one is the one whom I call The Witch, who constantly berates anything that I do. She's got wild hair and a red screaming face. This next is one that looks like me naked, like a recurrent dream I had when I was a kid in which I would go to school with no clothes on but didn't know it until halfway through the day. You know, I still often feel naked even with my clothes on—exposed to the world in terms of my inadequacies. And this third one is the Piggy—my overeating. And there's the food in the middle. So those are the few that I drew right away.

Man Participant: I have five separate pictures, but brother, are they ever dillies. The first one shows a wimp who is constantly repeating, "I'm not good enough. I'll never succeed. And I don't deserve to." The second—this gross huge character, who looks like Arnold Schwarzenegger on a bad day, is my bully. He works with the wimp to always make sure I get beaten up or taken whenever I try anything new. Here, in this third picture we have this nervous flealike fellow who is running away from a clock with jaws, a devouring clock, which is me always procrastinating so as not to have to accomplish anything. The fourth shows me with a hammer constantly breaking my own heart. I do that by dwelling on broken love affairs. And then the fifth looks like a Freudian analyst with a little goatee and glasses. He's always telling me that I have too many complexes and it will take me forever to get them sorted out. And you know what? He's right!

PART TWO

(After a break, the Guide will advise the participants to bring out their mushy food and to get into bathing suits or old clothes. Then all should cover the floor with a drop cloth or carry their cartoons and food outdoors in preparation for a grand melee. After this is done the Guide will say:)

Find a partner. Working in twos, begin to feed your toxic raiders. Put the mushy food on each of the pictures. While you do this, comment to your partner about the ways in which you emotionally and psychologically feed each of the raiders. For example, you might say, "This canned stew which I am pouring on the picture of this witch represents the ways in which I constantly feed her cauldron and allow myself to be stirred by all the nasty things she says to me. And I'm dumping these marshmallows on my piggy self, as well as this green jello and soft chocolate bars, because she has a compulsion to eat sweet and gooey things whenever she is feeling sorry for herself . . ." Your partner will then respond with commentary about the meaning of what she is feeding the pictures of her own toxic raiders. Make your statements as full of vehemence as you can. "Take that, you lazy bum!!!" Begin. (Ten minutes.)

Now stand back, look at the mess you have created in feeding your toxic raiders, and then walk around and view everybody else's mess. (Five minutes.)

I ask you now to return to your own pictures, pick up handfuls of the food, and hurl them at each other. Know that as you do this you are throwing away your tendency to feed your toxic raiders. As you throw the food from your pictures at each other, you might say words like, "I'm throwing away my need to feed the witch! Here, take this glop of oatmeal which stands for my feeding my piggy toxic raider!" You get the idea, and don't forget to laugh. And so BEGIN! (Five minutes.)

After this experience, which you will never forget, you will be remarkably conscious of each temptation to feed your raider whenever it arises, and you will be able to stop the negative or toxic thought or behavior before it gets nourished. After today, you have a good chance to starve all toxic raiders. Just remember what you have been through and say "stop" to the feeding. In this way you will find that you have gone off automatic response and entered into more conscious awareness of your thoughts and feelings. You are ready to contemplate the New Mind just as Deganawidah offered the woman his message of the New Mind after she had agreed to stop feeding the toxic raiders. But first, take a break, clean up the mess, and get cleaned up yourself as we prepare for Part Three.

(During the break the room or the place where the food fight took place will be cleaned up, the papers and garbage put into bags. People will wash and change and prepare the room for the next part in which a very large piece of paper or several medium sheets pasted or taped together is placed in the middle of the floor.)

PART THREE

Gathering together in a circle now around the large paper, hold hands, close your eyes, and begin to speak to each other about the kinds of things in your life, as well as the life of your family, community, profession, and the world that you would like to feed, to nourish. We have given up feeding the raiders; now let us name what we wish to nourish. Since we never want to stop offering food, the food of action and thought, it is important to discover to whom or to what we want to give sustenance. (Five minutes.)

Working together begin to make a collective drawing of what you have just expressed to each other. Draw it as pictures or symbols or even words. This will be the map of the possible human in the possible world—a world that Deganawidah himself expressed as one of right mind, right justice, and right health. As you do this, find ways to link your drawings and reflections to other people's drawings and reflections, creating the basis for a new order of healthy and creative community. (Thirty to forty-five minutes.)

(After all have finished, the Guide invites all to share in a feast of beautiful foods and music to honor the ending of the old toxic ways and the beginning of a new order of peace and creativity. Place the huge communal drawing on the wall or somewhere near the place of feasting and treat it like a sacred guest of honor, offering toasts and blessings to it.)

3

THE LONGHOUSE

Deganawidah's next challenge was to present to the woman a plan for a possible society so vital in its programs, so visionary and yet so concrete in it details, that it would serve as a lure of becoming. In fact, Deganawidah's vision encompassed the recreation of every aspect of communal life, as well as addressing the major issues that face all societies. But to begin, Deganawidah explained that his message was simple: "I speak for the Master of Life, and the word that I bring is that all people shall love one another and live together in peace." In this statement he offered a way to get beyond our negative habits and to welcome instead the consciousness that carries the Mind of the Maker. It may be that we cannot rid ourselves of the raiders completely, but we can expand our mind, nurture higher forces within it, and find that, as a consequence, we have stopped nurturing the forces of chaos and destruction.

Deganawidah's message had three equally vital aspects—*Gaiwoh, Skénon,* and *Gashasdénshaa,* which some tribal elders translate as righteousness, health, and power. *Righteousness* requires that individuals and nations establish the custom and expectation of justice between and among themselves and that they develop a deep willingness to see that justice is done. In our terms, Deganawidah was describing an ecology between cultures and peoples, a cooperative way of being in which no one is injured physically or psychologically. Instead, interactions between groups and individuals are cocreative and mutually nourishing.

Health establishes a sense of balance in body and mind and incorporates the inner peace which comes when bodies are nurtured and minds are free and at ease. The health Deganawidah was proposing was not simply the absence of dis-ease. Rather, he had in mind a kind of ebullience in the bones—an abundance of vitality and well-being.

In Deganawidah's great law of peace the word *power* implies autonomy, sovereignty, authority, and also authentic connection to spiritual dimensions and to the will of the Great Spirit. In reality Deganawidah was proposing what we might call "spiritual power," or *orenda* in the Mohawk language, a divine essence that unites all things. By tapping into *orenda*, the creative force of life, we find knowledge of appropriate laws and ways of being which lead to a better society. As human behavior improves, a new governance emerges, a spiritual politics in which true justice prevails. Moreover, by accessing *orenda*, we also tap into a larger pattern in which we are able to live out of the Greater Spirit rather than out of our own lesser one.

We can almost hear Deganawidah's deep and hesitant voice as he speaks the words that he has been considering for years. He invites us, first, to embrace a New Mind that looks fearlessly at our present conditions, seeing what is missing or deeply needed. For the people of Deganawidah's world, what was needed was active cocreation with the Mind of the Master of Life leading to a higher form of justice for all, with programs for healing and making whole every person's body and mind. As a means to this end, he envisioned councils that would engender dreams as well as discussion, visions as well as practical programs, to explore ways of bringing the patterns of heaven into earth. Such patterns are held in the creative Mind of Being, and they are also within ourselves. Deganawidah believed that open-minded discussion and mutual exploration spurred their rediscovery and thus inspired social and individual transformation.

The woman was deeply moved by the message, but she wondered what form these ideas would need to take in order to work in the world. It is then that the Peacemaker laid the matrix, the pattern upon which to build the new society. The Peacemaker explained further, using an analogy both homey and practical, that his ideas for bringing peace would take the form of the Longhouse. In the Longhouse, many families lived peaceably and to mutual advantage under one roof. Each family had its own fire and its own opening to the sky, but a single building offered protection to all. One chief mother held authority over all the families. In Deganawidah's vision, the five nations, Seneca, Onondaga, Mohawk, Cayuga, and Oneida, would form an extended polity. In this greater Longhouse of nations, each tribe would hold its own place, yet feel the power of the Confederacy stretching under and above them. Unity among them would be brought about by a life of peaceful trade instead of constant warfare. As the people of the Longhouse express it today, continuing the oral tradition of this story, Deganawidah told the woman: "They shall be the *Kanonsionni* [Extended House]. They shall have one deep mind and live under one deep law. Thinking shall replace killing, and there shall be one commonwealth."

The actual Longhouse building was a crucial concept in Deganawidah's plan and in the development of the new community he would forge. It is therefore helpful to know what a Longhouse was. To build one, a curved framework of sapling elm poles was constructed: it was sometimes as wide as 25 feet and as long as 125 feet. Covered with pieces of seasoned elm bark, with a rounded door at each end, a Longhouse looked somewhat like an overturned canoe some 20 feet high. There were no windows, but smoke holes were left open in the high roof, which could be closed with sliding panels when the rains and snows poured down. From ten to twenty families lived in a single Longhouse, each family sharing its fire with one other family. The fires were spaced some 12 feet apart. The building had space along the side for food storage and utensils, as well as huge bearskin-covered bunks for family sleeping. From the rafters hung ears of corn, squash, drying apples, tobacco, roots, and tubers. A family's space was acknowledged as personal and could be sheltered from other families by hangings or curtains.

The eldest woman in the Longhouse was the Mother. She and other women of the house "owned" the Longhouse. The families in each house were all related through clan lineages; when a man married, he entered his wife's lineage and her family Longhouse, with its clan symbol over the door. Each matrilineal family was thus part of a clan society. From the clans grew the moiety (or half-tribe); from the half-tribe grew the full tribe. Marriages were made between people of different clans, thus from outside any connection to the mother's blood kin. Children were born into their mother's clan. The intricate system of relationships under the roof of the Longhouse provided in their structure for an intensive communal life. In order to create the intertribal society he envisioned, Deganawidah built upon the engagement and emotional richness of a society in which the feminine and the family played vital roles.

Understanding something of the Iroquois system of agriculture and its relation to women's roles is also important. Women were responsible for the complex farming work of the tribe since, as bearers of children, they were recognized as holders of the earth's fertility. When women could have freedom to visit the fields outside the barricaded settlement without fear of raids and violence, an abundant society could grow.

In the world that Deganawidah inhabited, agriculture centered around what were called "the three sisters," corn, squash, and beans, but the Iroquois also cultivated many other vegetables and tended extensive orchards. In good times, the five tribes that eventually made up the Iroquois nation had a rich and varied diet, in which meat was less important than it was to peoples who focused more on hunting and fishing. Most of the major ceremonials of the Iroquois year were devoted to giving thanks for food planted, grown, or harvested; Thanksgiving celebrations marked the harvest in October, the rise of the maple sap in late February or March, the planting of corn in May or June; a strawberry festival welcomed the first fruit of the summer.

Women cultivated seventeen varieties of maize or corn. According to one estimate, in the Seneca tribe of about five thousand people, the women harvested a million bushels of corn every year. They also grew sixty varieties of beans and seven types of squashes. In addition, they collected thirty-four kinds of wild fruits, eleven species of nuts, six varieties of mushrooms, twelve types of edible roots, and thirty-eight varieties of bark, stem, and leaf products. This last, by the way, they collected from the trees only every other year or every two or three years to avoid damaging the trees by overharvesting. The Iroquois diet also included twelve beverages and eleven infusions from parts of plants used as occasional drinks and medicine. Salt was not a staple; maple sap, however, was used to flavor cornmeal, sweeten mush, and as a beverage.[1] Thus before the Europeans came and burned and pillaged their lands (under the pretense that these native peoples were only hunters, never farmers), the peoples of the eastern woodlands had one of the highest dietary standards in the known world, and many lived to advanced age. A life span of a hundred or so years was not uncommon.

What had happened before Deganawidah's time to cause such hardship, chaos, and destruction cannot be fully known. It is an enigma lost in mist like the sudden disappearance of the Anasazi people in the Southwest. We do know that planting beans with corn, as the Iroquois did, helps to restore nutrients to the soil, and controlled burning techniques can keep land productive for a long period of time; nevertheless, every fifteen or twenty years, a Longhouse settlement was forced to move into fresh territory because the land had worn out. Perhaps the push for more land helped create the tensions which brought about the preconfederacy conditions of social unrest and warfare.

Deganawidah's gift was the ability to see a way of fostering inter-tribal cooperation to relieve the tensions and restore the healthful conditions he knew could prevail when people worked together in a fertile and abundant land. He proposed, in effect, a multinational Longhouse community, with the traditional building serving as both symbol and microcosm of the larger community of nations. The intertribal Longhouse would extend from the Hudson River valley in what is now southern New York state up to the Genesse River in the northwest, a distance of some three hundred miles. A Great Longhouse indeed! Whether Deganawidah chose the Longhouse as his pattern for a unified nation because the people already saw themselves as builders of unique houses, or whether they became so after his time, to this day people of the region call themselves *Haudenosaunee*, People of the Longhouse or House Builders, in recognition and celebration of this distinguishing feature of their civilization.

After hearing Deganawidah describe his vision and the primary thoughts, symbols, and patterns upon which it could manifest, the woman acknowledged its allure and power. Tradition holds that she replied to Deganawidah in ceremonial language: "That is indeed a good message. I take hold of it. I embrace it." These words illustrate that agreement should be an active process. When we come across an idea that speaks deeply to us and we agree to work for it, we must literally bring it into our bodies, taking hold of it, incorporating it, embracing it with acceptance and love. Because she was the first to hear his message and fully engage her life to it, Deganawidah named her *Jigonhsasee*, which means New Face, because her face showed forth the New Mind. He further told her that in the Longhouse of the five nations, women would hold the title and power of chiefs. She herself would be called the Mother of Nations and be known as the Great Peacewoman who would help bring the Good Tidings of Peace and Power.

It feels important to pause and think about why the legend tells us that the first person to embrace the Mind of the Maker, as described by Deganawidah, should be a woman. Records of the Iroquois League illustrate clearly the role women played, not only in the Longhouse community, in agriculture, and in child-raising, but also in the political system. Women made proposals, often originating them, chose the male sachems (chiefs), guided and counseled them, and when necessary, replaced them. Moreover, women were seen as the wise ones and the spiritual heads of the tribes. Clearly, native women, particularly among the Iroquois, were extremely hard working, but they also participated in the lives of their people much more fully and with much greater respect than white women did during the same period.

Later stories tell us that, in many cases, when Colonial girl children raised in Indian settlements had the opportunity to return to white culture, they refused; whereas, Indian girls raised by whites always returned to the tribe, if they were allowed to. A famous example of the former was reported by James Madison, who traveled up the Mohawk River and discovered a white woman living among the Oneidas. She told him that as a young girl she had been a servant in a wealthy home in New York. While still in adolescence she had run away and gone to live with the Iroquois. Welcomed by the Oneidas, she had lived with them in a very happy state ever since. She told Madison further that there was simply no advantage to living as a white woman in a white world. As she put it:

> . . . the whites treated me harshly. I saw them take rest while they made me work without a break. I ran the risk of being beaten, or dying of hunger, if through fatigue or laziness I refused to do what I was told. Here, I have no master, I am the equal of all the woman of the tribe, I do what I please without anyone saying anything about it. I work only for myself,—I shall marry if I wish and be unmarried again when I wish. Is there a single woman as independent as I in your cities?[2]

But for me, no evidence about the importance of women to the tribe is stronger than the story of Deganawidah. Before he could face his most dramatic challenges, before he could truly begin his mission, Deganawidah had to lay out and discuss the details of his vision with a woman and gain her understanding and approval. Only when she was persuaded of the truth and importance of his message, could he go forward. In some other ways this story is similar to those of heroes and savior figures of the European and Middle Eastern cultures, but the presence and the actions of Jigonhsasee make this legend unique. It is she who blesses the message, and it is her lodge which becomes the center of the New Mind.

Like Jigonhsasee, Mother of Nations, we too can see the logic and the beauty of Deganawidah's message of love and peace. To stop feeding our own raiders, we can expand our minds by entering the Mind of the Maker. Let me explain further what this means.

The purpose of any great culture of spirit like the one brought into being through this story is to provide a multitude of ways for its members to come to a deepened sense of the High Self, the place within where the Maker of and Participant in all Things resides. A culture of spirit asks the local, everyday, going-to-work, bill-paying self to be willing to serve as a worthy member of the High Self's crew. When the local self is in a state of profound integration with the High Self, it will always be richer for the experience and more deeply aware of the permutations and nuances of life. This is so because the High Self is itself a resonance of the Creative Power of the universe, which I call the Mind of the Maker.

How do we do this? How do we align our own creative capacities with the Creator in ways which do not burn us out but serve, rather, to grow and green our world? How do we learn to see and hear and feel our way into the Mind of the Maker and, in so doing, add to the health and vitality of those around us, renew our spirits, and give us a deepened sense of our life's purpose and the courage to heal what has been hurt, replenish what has been exhausted, and redeem, in T. S. Eliot's beautiful phrase, "the unread vision of the higher dream"? Each of us carries the creative spark which can restore our world and its living things to a new wholeness. Perhaps the most critical question of our time is, how do we prepare ourselves to participate in the New Creation? The process that follows this chapter will suggest a number of ways to begin.

NOTES

[1] William Sturtevant, *The Native Americans, Indigenous People of North America* (New York: Smithmark Publishers, 1991), p. 231.

[2] Quoted in Donald A. Grinde, Jr., "Iroquois Political Concepts and the Genesis of American Government," in *Indian Roots of American Democracy*, Jose Barreiro, ed. (Ithaca, NY: Akwe:Kon Press, Cornell University, 1992), p. 52.

ENTERING THE MIND OF THE MAKER

TIME: Ninety minutes.

MATERIALS: None.

MUSIC: Drumming and pow wow music. Space music if desired.

INSTRUCTIONS FOR GOING SOLO: This exercise lends itself wonderfully well to the solo journey. Just make sure that you give yourself sufficient pauses as you make the tape of the script for the Guide.

We are on the verge of an extraordinary understanding of the way things work and what we humans can be in this expanding universe. We are reaching with tentative fingers to touch and be touched by the hand and mind of the Maker. Great sages, wise women, and creative minds of the past have felt this touch. But now the metaphors which help us to understand and express what is happening are growing richer, and that makes it possible for a wider range of people to experience the Mind of the Maker. For now we venture out through space and time in the macrocosm of galaxies and other universes, investigating quantum fields and primal cosmic forces. At the same time, our imaginations and technologies are also allowing us to spiral into the microcosm, toward subatomic infinities wherein we see the universe in miniature. We study and reflect upon these miracles and mysteries, hoping to fathom the vastness expanding in both directions, as well as the fragile balancing point between them, which is ourselves.

Part of the miracle is that we each seem to contain family history, cultural and even species memory, as well as codings from the very unfolding of evolution, and even the patterns of the great charge that started it all in those initial moments of the birth of the universe. I suspect that the present emerging ecology of mind, culture, and psyche indicates that, in some mysterious way, we are being rescaled to planetary proportions, as we become more resonant and intimate with our own depths and with the deep ecology of the Earth Herself. We are being prepared now, as in Deganawidah's time, for sacred stewardship and responsibility for planetary governance. We are moving more and more into the Mind of the Maker. We are being invited to become partners of creation.

To aid this process, we embark here upon an exercise in which we attempt to identify a number of the systems and functions of our brain and mind with the Mind of the Maker and with the creative energy of evolution that brought all things into being.

Before beginning, let us review some of the recent studies concerning brain parts and their functions. We find some of the most fascinating and relevant brain research in the work of Paul MacLean and his associates. MacLean, who was formerly chief of the Laboratory of Brain Evolution and Behavior at the National Institute of Mental Health, has presented evidence that our neurological equipment has evolved over time into what he calls the triune brain. This name refers to the three major neural systems which emerged sequentially in evolutionary history, through which we inherit the many developments of the species which preceded us and, perhaps, the latent potential which is yet to unfold.

In effect, we contain three brains, which evolved from the earliest reptilian brain, through the paleomammalian system of our old animal brain, to our present human neomammalian brain. These three brains operate in a nested fashion, with the reptilian or R-complex brain providing the foundation for the more advanced structures of the old mammalian and the new mammalian brains to build upon. Each of these brains continues to have its own specific tasks to perform as well as its own characteristic behaviors.

For example, in the recesses of the reptilian brain, we contain the fish, the reptile, and the amphibian, who still to some extent govern our survival attitudes as well as those patterns that call for maintenance of habit and stability. Responsible for our sensory-motor system as well as for those physical processes that keep us awake and aware in the world, the reptilian brain is also our automatic pilot and stores those learnings about operating in the world that comes to us from higher brain functions. We can blame our reptile when we get into obsessive-compulsive behaviors or a tiresome devotion to details and routines, but we can thank our reptile when we realize that it provides sufficient unconscious protection to help us maintain stability within an ever-changing world. Being ancient within us, the reptilian brain also provides us with our primary energy and our life-support systems.

The second brain to develop, the paleomammalian brain, contains the midbrain and limbic system (from *limb*, which means "to wrap around"). Not only does the limbic system wrap around the reptilian brain, but it offers a far more adaptable and inventive intelligence, as well as many more openings to the nature and function of reality. Within it continues to survive something of the herd of mammalian beasts and their prodigious preparations for partnership and procreation, which in turn gives us the emotional impetus for the development of family, clan, and the early basis for civilization. This brain, therefore, contains the cranial endocrine glands that govern sexual development, sleep, dreams, desire, pleasure, and pain—the full spectrum of emotional life. It is the seat of intuition and grounds the fantasies and inventiveness that comes from its relative above, the neocortex. But since it also works to combine the three brains, it can direct the intellectual powers of our highest brain into service of the lower brain's defense system in an emergency, whether real or imagined.

Dangerous as well as desirous, this early mammalian brain also contains the neurochemistry that makes for war, aggression, violence, dominance, and alienation. When activated and amplified, this part of the brain can be experienced by the unprepared as inflation of the ego and a stupendous emotional passion for willing one's way. In the person who works on herself, however, the result is just the opposite, for it also can give one a deep sense of compassion for all beings—what the Buddhists call the bodhisattva mind. In this state one may have tremendous power, but one uses it to serve others, rather than to control them.

The third and most recently developed brain is the neomammalian, consisting of the neocortex and frontal lobes. The neocortex is divided into right and left hemispheres, each of which is thought to have its own specialties. The left hemisphere is concerned with temporal, linear, objective, analytic data processing, language, and logic, while the right is more involved with visual, spatial, intuitive, subjective, and analogical thinking. These parts of the brain, the last to develop and five times larger than the earlier two brains, work in an integrated manner to control conscious thought and activities: reason, will, analysis, logic, calculation, voluntary movement, creativity and, when developed, altruism, empathy, identity, compassion, and higher orders of love. The frontal lobes are involved in the development of the visionary and the higher mind, the mind that can enter into causality itself. The activation of this newest brain, with its enormous powers of reflection and self-awareness, allows for the integration and conscious orchestration of the other brains. It thus can use the simpler systems of the earlier neural structures for its own higher purposes. Part a cold, calculating computer, part a home for paradox and a vehicle of transcendence, the neocortex is that aspect of ourselves that determines whether as a species we will grow or die.

Moreover, the neocortex is the part of the brain more given to higher frequency patterns. This means that in states of deep meditation or contemplation, certain spiritual exercises, high creativity, mystical or unitive experience, this part of the brain enters into a frequency resonance with higher orders of reality—even, we suspect, with those higher creative forces which we are calling the Mind of the Maker. It is, thus, more connected to the realms of psyche and, thus, is possibly the neurological doorway to the great archetypal and creative patterns of existence. It has a capacity to tap the source levels, to hear the music of the spheres, and to see the architecture of creation and consciousness.

SCRIPT FOR THE GUIDE:

We are about to employ a metaphor in which the four areas of the brain are seen as reflections of the Mind of the Maker. We will consider the right hemisphere of the neocortex as that aspect of the Creator's mind that imagines the whole of creation and the left hemisphere as the activating, name and form-giving, detail-seeking power of the creative process. We will invite the limbic system of the brain to reflect the feelings and emotional associations concerning creation, while the R-complex with its capacity for survival and deep rootedness will find identity—oneness—with all that is created.

Begin to walk now, with your eyes softly closed or half-closed. As you walk, focus your attention on the right hemisphere of your brain and, at the same time, begin to make circles with your eyes, as if they were traveling through the right hemisphere of your brain. Just circle with your eyes and, at the same time, move or dance. You are making circles on the right part of your brain while your eyes are closed and moving or dancing at the same time. Making circles with your closed eyes and breathing deeply, with the intention of sending fresh oxygen into the brain. Breathing into the Mind of the Maker. Breathing into the mind of the Holder of Heaven . . .

Now focusing on the left hemisphere of the brain, breathe into it, while you make circles with your closed or half-closed eyes on the left hemisphere of the brain. Circling and circling with your eyes inside your head, while you move and dance with your body . . .

And now let your eyes follow the path of the corpus collosum, the part of the brain that connects the two hemispheres of the neocortex. Think of it as a long path; much information and trade travels between the sides of the brain linked by the corpus collosum . . . Without the corpus collosum the two sides of the brain and their functions would never get together . . . Allowing your eyes to follow the great connecting path of the corpus collosum . . .

Let your eyes move back and forth now throughout the regions of your brain, uniting and strengthening the pathway between the two brains, the two hemispheres of the neocortex, the road which connects the two brains, the path of peace and of integration. This is the path that connects the ecology of your brain's mind. Feed it with light as your eyes circle and move along the path. Circling, circling through the middle of the brain, to the top, and then down and under, and then up to the top, and right down the center of your head . . .

Now feel as if a sky hook has grabbed the top of your hair and is pulling you gently upward. Your body now moves in its gentle dance around a center line. As you imagine this, make circles with your eyes, focusing attention on the center of the head, the section that is called the midbrain. This is the limbic system, with a vast pharmacopeia of enzymes and hormones that, among other things, create and sustain the emotions of the brain . . . Continuing to make circles with your eyes, focusing attention on the limbic system . . . Have a sense that as you continue to circle, you are bringing the light of the Mind of the Maker to nourish and sustain your emotional being. You may even feel a surge of emotional energy, of quickened vitality, a palette of desire, yearning, happiness, sadness, wonder, astonishment . . .

Now focus your attention toward the back of your head. In your dance and movement, slowly move your head forward, lowering your chin toward your chest, and then lift it up and back so that your chin points to the sky hook that is helping to pull you gently toward the heavens. Bring your attention to the back of your head and your spine, home of the most ancient brain, sometimes called the reptilian brain . . . And allow your eyes to continue to circle, but this time focused there in the oldest part of your brain, the R-complex, that monitors your mechanisms of survival. Located there in the inside and lower part of the back of the head, it is the part of you that loves the drum, loves ritual, loves repetition, loves rhythm. (A Native American drumming tape begins here.)

So let that part of the brain enjoy the sound of the drum. And let the drum bring light into your brain as your eyes circle through the reptilian complex. And move your spine a little, because the spinal cord is part of that brain. Let your spine move to the rhythm of the drumbeat.

And now with your eyes circle through the entire brain. Weave great spirals, galactic spirals of light and energy through the whole brain. The eyes circling, cycling through the brain as the drumbeat accompanies this journey. Create the sense now that the sky hook connecting you to the heavens is providing an opening to the Mind of the Creator, the Mind of the Maker, an opening of light and energy . . . Begin circling horizontally with your eyes at the same level as your eyes, but spiraling inward until you reach the very center in the middle of your brain where it is too small to circle, and just rest your attention there. If you lose that central place, just start spiraling horizontally with your eyes inward until you reach that place in the middle where it is too small for circling . . . And all the time breathing and breathing into that center place. Breathing into it so it seems to become warm. Then hot. It becomes fiery; a pulsing fiery point like the hydrogen atom at the moment of the Big Bang that launched creation. (Space music starts here if the Guide chooses.)

And then suddenly fling your head around and around, breathing that tremendous great initial charge of creation—CHOOM!—known as the Big Bang. The Mind of the Creator! The Mind of the Maker! Breathing deeply into the whole brain as it recapitulates those early moments of creation. And going very rapidly through the evolution of the universe, the high energy flux of atoms in the heat wave of the early universe, the eventual cooling and bonding of atoms and molecules and the formation of matter, matter that turned into stars, into planets, into life—all contained within the Mind of the Maker; all contained in your own skull space. For know that you are part of the metabolism of the galaxy, the Creator's mind rendered concrete and human.

Now we will explore some of the reflections and dimensions of this mind. (Drumming tape begins again, softly.) From the Mind of the Maker (as you continue to move) would you please have the sense that you can create the idea of APPLE. Then begin to paint, sculpt, form, or feel on the right side of the brain a drenched and dripping APPLE TREE in an orchard of apple trees stretching to infinity. From the Mind of the Creator into your mind and body, a world of "drenched and dripping" apple trees. Imagine it and then create it with your hands. See it inside the right brain—great fertile, fecund, drenched and dripping, huge, ebullient, fruiting apple trees.

Create it on the right brain. Form it in your hands. Dance it so that you become those dancing, dripping branches and their round red fruits . . .

And from the Mind of the Creator now on the left side of the brain, would you see, feel, sculpt, create a beautiful perfect single RED APPLE. Perfection itself. See it there in its fullness and beauty, its exquisite detail. The shading of colors, the texture of the skin, its connection to the tree . . . On the left side of the brain, forming it, seeing it, perhaps even being it. Touch it, and know what it feels like to be touched as if you were an apple. Move with the sense of individual perfection of one apple.

Now would you let the idea of apple move into the emotional part of your brain so that you can smell it. Our sense of smell feeds directly into the limbic brain. Would you then from that place begin to sense your emotional connections to apple—dunking for apples on Halloween, Mom's apple pies. Recalling, perhaps, the temptation of Eve to taste an apple. Let the emotional associations rise. The apple in your bag lunch that you took to school. Offering a friend a bite from your apple. "Apple core; Baltimore! Who's your friend?" . . . "I will give my love an apple, without any core . . ." Let there rise in you memories and associations and emotional connections to apple. Feel yourself move with these emotions around the idea of apple . . .

Now drop back to the oldest brain you have, located at the back of the skull, the old reptilian complex. Invite attention to focus back there, as if your eyes could see this part of your brain . . . Take a bite out of this imaginal apple and, as the juice unites with your sense of taste, let this union of human and apple lead you to an awareness of becoming one with that ground of being that makes it possible for an apple tree to grow. Let your body feel itself to be the ground around the tree. And from within the ground feel the driving pulse of lifebeat urging you to live and grow and be the fullness of what is coded within you. A being for all seasons. Become rooted and covered with bark, a great rooted blossomer, deeply rooted with branches reaching up to heaven and spreading across the horizon. Dying back in wintertime but eternally returning every spring . . .

Buffeted by winds, weather, by rains and snow and searing sun, but always continuing to bud and flower, to make fruit and let fall your apples, your gifts of life and new beginnings . . .

Now in your whole brain, allow all of these phases to be present. The great trees in general and each individual apple. All of the emotional connections with apple. All of the stages in the life of the apple tree. All the seasons in the year. The ground on which it is rooted. The sky to which its branches reach. So that through the whole brain, you are able to hold many different images of this representative of the PLANT KINGDOM. And let yourself open to the joy of the Creator who says, "I take hold of it. I embrace it. It is good."

Now begin again to walk around, and bring your attention once more to the right brain. Search through the right brain and its pathways of light for the idea, the dream, of STONE. Then begin to see or feel all the possibilities of creating STONE, all the things stone can do, all the ways stone can be used, the great power you as Creator can sense in stone. Now in that great right hemisphere, the home of associational thinking, allow yourself to imagine impossible things made of stone, a stone newspaper, a stone heart, even, perhaps, a STONE CANOE . . .

Then on the left side of the brain, sense your ability to carve out and make a very particular stone canoe. Choose the special stone; see its details of color and hardness and shape. Then sense your hands chipping away at the stone, chipping, chipping away. Feeling the chipped block and the tiny chips of stone as they fall away. Hearing the sounds your hand tools make as you focus on the precision of your work carving out this stone canoe. All of this on the left hemisphere of your brain . . .

And in the emotional brain, the midbrain, gather emotional power around the creation of stone itself and all the beings of stone. Pebbles, canoes, rocks, cliffs, statues, crystals, jewels, stony mountains, granite caves. Discover now your emotional connections with the stone kingdom—Stone Age ancestors, "The Flintstones"; spelunking in caves; strolling on agate beaches; the great masons and sculptors building cathedrals, temples, carving statues; "Let he who is without sin cast the first stone"; diamonds, opals, emeralds, moonstones, sapphires, rubies. Emotions and memories about stone . . .

Allow yourself now to focus on the ancient brain and feel yourself becoming stone. You are one with stone. You have always been stone. You've been stone for millions of years. Perhaps you're a lighter stone than when you began, but you are stone. You know the eternity of stone and of being stone, the surety, the habituation of being stone and its diamond essence . . .

And then with the Mind of the Creator, the Mind of the Maker, be all of these at once—creating stone; imagining the impossible idea of a stone canoe; carving and chipping out a specific stone canoe; all emotional associations with stones, caverns, mountains, stone beings; then becoming stone itself. And breathe into the MINERAL KINGDOM. Breathe into it throughout your brain. You are the Creator of stone. You are stone, and you are the Creator of stone. And you look at it, and you think, "I take hold of it. I embrace it. It is good!"

(The Guide raises the volume on the drumming tape.)

Now let the drums rise as once again you begin to dance. And on the right side of your brain, begin to imagine the idea of ANIMAL. Create a world of animals. Many animals. Call them all into being. Design them in their essence; imbue them with qualities—strength, vitality, courage, cunning, a genius for living in the world. The soul power of the ANIMAL KINGDOM. The Mind of the Maker calling that kingdom into creation with the right hemisphere of the brain. See yourself as that Maker, that Creator of the world of animals.

On the left side of the brain, now see or sense some particular animal, one special animal. Focus the great power of the left hemisphere on the details of that animal. Hear its sounds, its songs and cries, yelps and howls. Notice in precise detail how it moves, runs, slithers, hides, fights, loves. Feel its skin, its fur, hide, claws, hooves, feathers. Let your body imitate its movements. Dance the dance of that animal. Feel furry and snouted and tufted and clawed and hoofed and tailed.

Focus now on the midbrain, the emotional brain, inviting in all of your associations with that animal—what it means to you, its totemic power. Feel both your emotions about this animal and its own emotional associations: its many realities, its memories, its home place on the planet, its environment—its trees, grasses, watering places, dens, nests—its life in community, its bornings, its dyings, its care for its young, its feedings, its huntings, its hidings, its very being.

And moving now to the ancient brain, the old brain in the back of the head, let yourself be one with the very soul and essence of that animal, so much so that its ways of moving are your ways, and you've known them thousands of years. Know its ways of protecting itself and its young as if they were your ways; nestle into the places of its deepest safety—they have always been yours. Its life flame is vital and strong, and you are one with it in this part of your brain that knows the deepest and oldest connection to the life force.

And then let yourself be suffused with the Mind of the Maker through the whole brain so that you create the animal on the right; you experience it on the left; you feel and enjoy and associate with all its family and relationships to the world in the midbrain; and you are that animal forever in the old brain. You are all these things, and you are within the Mind of the Maker. And you say, "I take hold of it. I embrace it. It is good!" (The Guide lowers the volume on the tape.)

And now on the right brain, imagine the creation of YOURSELF. See and begin to dance the idea of your life, from the time you were considered, say, a year before you were born. Join the great Pattern Keepers and Peacemakers saying, "This man or this woman shall be! This is a good idea, needed now in the late twentieth century on this planet!" And see or sense the whole picture, the great patterns of your life: being conceived and being born, being called into being, being created through food, through nourishment, through love, through empathy, through culture, through disappointment, through abuse, through wonder, through astonishment, through grace. Growing up from a child to an adolescent to an adult to the person you are now. See yourself being called into being and called now into your fullness, as you sense that life on the right hemisphere of your brain. And dance that life.

Now on the left brain, see or sense particulars of your life. See or experience yourself as a small image inside the left brain being carried in the large image of the whole body. Feel the details of that image: size, color of eyes, hair, skin. Use X-ray vision to see within, the blood and lymph flow, the bones, nerves, muscles, organs, glands of this particular you. See yourself in all your parts, not only in your physical body but also the specific condition of the life fields around your physical body. What does your emotional body look like? Is it a special color? How about your mental and spiritual bodies? Where do they reside? Keep scanning with the great inward camera of the left hemisphere to look for more and richer details of all these bodies. All your beings, all sheathed one upon the other—this complex entity called yourself.

Let the drums rise. (The Guide raises the volume of the tape.) Now focusing in the midbrain, the emotional center, the limbic system, experience all your associations—wild, wondrous, strange, terrifying, glorious—of being you and of being human. Feel the dominant emotion of this life: Is it joy? Excitement? Pleasure? Melancholy? Anger? Love? Add, like pieces of music, the tenderness, surges, counterpoint, harmonics of emotional life that enrich it and give it color and vibration. Dance the emotions of this vivid life . . .

Allow yourself to focus now on the old brain. As you do so, let your boundaries feel they can dissolve, and you become all human beings, every one. You are diaphanous to every human being who ever was, who is, or shall be. You are humanity itself. You are one with the urge to live, to be alive. You are one with all the dreams of humans. You feel yourself taking part in humankind's rituals of becoming. You feel within you the pulses and heartbeats that mark the inner rhythms and rituals of living. And at the same time, you know yourself to be one with the Mind of the Maker. You are the incarnation of the Mind of the Maker. You are all HUMANITY, ubiquitous through time and space with all who were, and are, and shall be. The Mind of the Maker in all humanity . . .

And you are able to hold it all. On the right brain, the pattern of your life in its entirety; on the left brain, the image of your body with all its sheathings; in the emotional brain, the spill of all your associations, emotions, relationships; and in the ancient brain, the human species present here and now. All of this at once. And loud and clear, say with me, "I take hold of it. I embrace it. It is good. I take hold of it. I embrace it. It is good. I take hold of it. I embrace it. It is good." (The Guide lowers the volume.)

And now begin to move or dance again, as we travel toward the creation and reflection of SPIRITUAL REALITIES. I ask you to focus once more on the right hemisphere of the brain. First imagine the idea and then perceive the creation of creation itself. The creation of the great patterns of creation, the creation of the patterns for making life, the codes for the DNA, the plans for stars and starfish, for glaciers and galaxies, and yes, the creation of philosophical and spiritual ideas. Here are created the laws of form. How are they formed? Or were they always there? Let that be the dreaming of the right brain, entering what the Australian aborigines call the Dreamtime, the place and time beyond place and time, the origins of creation by the great archetypal beings, told and sung to us in song and story: Yahweh blowing upon the void. Purusha dividing himself and becoming all of creation. Brahma dreaming the universe. Spider Woman weaving the worlds. Let your body dance these visions of the right brain . . .

Now move your attention to the left brain. There begin to see or sense the possibilities of specific spiritual realities. What shall these be named? How may they be experienced? Is it a notion of God, or Spirit, or the Mind behind it all? Allow it to form in the left brain. Is this spiritual creation a gassy essence? How does it manifest itself through many different forms? Is it a Christ figure or a Buddha? Is it a notion of Nirvana? Is it the Great Universal Mind? The Great Mother? Whatever it is, it is there in that left brain as it is known or has been known to you. And you breathe into it. Shape it. Dance with it. See it. Feel it, in a multitude of possible forms. Or perhaps it is known through relationships, the spirit between two people.

Perhaps it's in a child's eyes. Perhaps it is some noble and glorious work of art or music. Perhaps it is a perfect spring day. Perhaps it is some quality of love. But it is Spirit rendered in myriad forms. See it clearly with the left brain, on the left brain, in the left brain . . .

And go back even further to Being itself. Being itself emanating out of love into form, into creation. The love that moves the sun and all the stars. And then let that love just pour down from that Creator, from that Spiritual Force and all its emanations. Let that love pour down and suffuse and meet the love that's rising up from your own emotional center. Let there be love there, and let the loves meet and play together in the limbic system of your brain. And let there be there many of the feelings and thoughts you have associated with the Creative Spirit, your fear of God, your search for God—your yearning for God and for spiritual union . . .

Now as you dance, let your boundaries dissolve so that you no longer know whether you are the Dancer, the Dancing, or the Danced. The Doer, the Doing, or the Done. Feel yourself dissolving into no thing, and then resolving into one great Reality—the Mind of the Maker. With this dance of union, we are once again in the most ancient brain, where it is possible to know eternity. Sense how the categories of your local time are extended by the dimensions of a spiritual eternity that has always been and will always be—it just goes on and on and on. Time past, time future, gathered in time present. The eternal beingness.

And now with your entire mind, experience all possible manifestations of spirit and let them dance together. Imagine and sense the creative archetypes, their symbols, their patterns. The worlds of spiritual creations: of gods, stories, myths, and legends. Then invite them to share their knowings. Mix and match in the archetypal world. Let Queen Isis do lunch with Eagle Woman. Have Athena share her weavings with Spider Woman, her music with Saraswati. Bring about a meeting between Deganawidah and Mahatma Gandhi. All this on the right brain.

Then let rise within you images of all things great and small that partake of a spiritual essence—with dogs and apple pies and stone canoes and snow shoes and winking eyes and rabbits scampering through the grass . . . Now add your own spirit creations. Let your left brain call them into being . . . And enjoy the sweet union and communion of it all in the limbic center . . . Now sense the utter eternity of it all beyond space and time in the old brain, and hold this all together where there is only the Dance. (The Guide raises the volume.)

The drums rise again. And hold the Great Dance, the Mind of the Maker. And speak out the words of affirmation, "I take hold of it. I embrace it. It is good. I hold it. I embrace it. It is good. I hold it. I embrace it. It is good. I hold it. I embrace it. It is good. I hold it. I embrace it. It is good." The creation of apples. The apple. The creation of minerals. The stones and stone canoes. The animals of all species. Humanity. All human beings. The Spirit that informs it all. The Great Spirit. "I hold it. I embrace it. It is good."

(Pow Wow music is played.)

And it becomes the Pow Wow of All Beings. Dance now into the center of the room. I hold it. I embrace it. It is good. The Heart and the Mind of the Maker, replacing the mind that feeds the raider. And with this, then, receiving, taking whatever is your deep form of knowing what for you and for the larger community can be health, can be soundness and depth of mind, can be justice and the creation of new forms of communities, of cooperation, can be the creation of appropriate law and governance, can be the tapping into spiritual potency, spiritual power, and the right use of this depth of power for yourself, for your community, for your world. The Mind of the Maker. The Mind of the Peacemaker. . . . And as the music plays, dance and express these things. (Five to ten minutes.)

(After the dance the Guide gathers everyone into the center and says:)

And as you have experienced and known much in what we have just celebrated together, please feel free to say something about what you have felt and seen and known. These are mysteries, but they are ones that can be shared. So please share your vision. Tell us of what you have seen, and how it can be used to help us find a New Mind and Spirit for ourselves and our world. (Open discussion and sharing period.)

This has been an exercise honoring Deganawidah and the codings of the new orders, the new possibilities, the new potencies of peace. Peace as a greening; peace that ameliorates the ways of hate, that energizes deeper knowings in very practical ways, that pulses through our bloodstream, our heartbeat, our knowings, and that calls us to the remembrance of who and what we really are, so that we can do the impossible—dream the impossible dream and then go out and do something about it. It is the empowerment of dust. It is the insistence that bursts up from the mud. It is creation. HO!

NOTE

1 I discuss the theory of the triune brain in my book *The Possible Human* (Los Angeles: Jeremy Tarcher, Inc., 1982), pp. 99–104. Paul Maclean's works can be found in any number of his scientific papers. The most important for this discussion is "On the Evolution of Three Mentalities," in *New Dimensions in Psychiatry: A World View* (Vol. 2), edited by Silvano Arieti and Gerard Chrynowski (New York: Wiley, 1977).

4

GO TOWARD THE SUNRISE

We are at the place in the story when Jigonhsasee, now called the Great Peacewoman and Mother of Nations, has accepted the message of Deganawidah, saying, "I take hold of it. I embrace it." What is the message of this event? Deganawidah, as we recall, was not accepted among his own people. He set out on his impossible mission completely alone. Wisely, he was willing to work with anyone who would listen. It is as if he had said, "I will go through the world until I find those who can hear me, who can be part of this new dream. I will take on a larger circle of allies." Jigonhsasee was the first of these new allies. We, too, must be willing to speak the new truth as we understand it, without fear of being misunderstood or rejected, and with the confidence that the right allies will hear us clearly, embrace us and our message, and come to our aid.

Now Jigonhsasee asked Deganawidah, "Where will you take your message next?"

"I go toward the sunrise. I go to the new," he replied.

"That direction is dangerous," she told him. "A cannibal lives on the path that leads to the sunrise."

The sunrise always is dangerous. The sunset is less so, because it stands for the old ways and expectations. Moving toward the sunset can symbolize retreating into old habits, contracted attitudes, and tunnel vision. I use the term "sunset effect" to describe what happens when the old ways flare out with great authority, majesty, and power, like the sun in the western sky, before eventually sinking beneath the horizon of history and culture. The sunrise, on the other hand, is unpredictable and sometimes precarious. It is a place of ambiguities, of intense light suddenly careening into fearful shadows, like the shadow of cannibalism, the particular danger that lay along the path that Deganawidah had chosen.

Undaunted, Deganawidah replied, "That is what I am here to change; I am here to end such evils so that all paths become open and safe for everyone."

Deganawidah then traveled to the lodge where the cannibal lived. Looking around, he saw that the man was not there, so he climbed up onto the low roof of the dwelling and lay down next to the opening in the roof used for smoke to escape. Eventually, the eater of human flesh returned, dragging a freshly killed human corpse. He filled a huge kettle with water and set it over the fire, adding his gruesome dinner to the pot. Deganawidah shifted his body and deliberately looked down through the smoke hole into the water of the kettle.

When the cannibal approached to stir his pot, he looked into the water and saw a face reflected in the water looking back at him. He was stunned by the face. Not realizing he was seeing Deganawidah, the cannibal thought he was seeing himself. And what a face! Strength, forbearance, character, even wisdom, shone forth from the face he saw reflected.

He pulled back and sat down to think. His face, but also a True Face, the face of a noble and good being. "That's a great man looking out at me from the kettle," he said to himself. "I had not realized I looked like that. That is a face of goodness. That is not the face of a man who eats other people." He began to think about his situation, about who he really was and what he had become. This is the dawn of the New Mind: willingness to look fearlessly at what we have created of our lives.

After a while, doubts arose, and he began to wonder if he had really seen the face he thought he saw. Cautiously, he approached the kettle for a second look. The steadfast Deganawidah was still up on the roof, peering down the smoke hole into the kettle, and so the noble face was still looking up at the cannibal from the water.

"It is me!" cried the cannibal. "It is! That's really me! How about that? That is a tremendous person. That's a great man. That's not the face of a man who eats humans. What am I going to do with this soup? I'd better dump it."

Once he acknowledged the truth of his True Face, the cannibal realized that he could no longer act as he had acted, without conscience, mindfulness, or compassion. Struck with remorse, he took action immediately. He carried the kettle with its human stew out into the forest, burying it in the space left by the roots of an overturned tree. (In a forest culture, you always seem to have an uprooted tree where you can get rid of things.)

Then he sat there, overcome with the grief and shock of self-awareness. "All right. I've changed my habits. I am no longer a cannibal. But now my conscience is torturing me because of all the evil I have done and the suffering I have caused." These reflections made him very morose, and he fell into an agony of guilt. In his shame, he said aloud, "I wish someone would come along to tell me how to make amends to all the human beings that I wronged. I wish there were someone who could show me a way of relieving my pain at having hurt others so badly. Is there any way I can take actions that will make up for the dreadful things I have done?"

These thoughts reflect the basic Native American idea of balancing evil deeds with right action. Evil cannot be erased, of course, but doing good can help redress inequities in both the earth and ourselves. Thinking these thoughts, the man made his way back to his house. Standing there waiting for him was Deganawidah. Still puzzling over the day's events, the former cannibal invited his guest into the lodge and restored the fire; then the two sat facing each other across the flames.

Filled with wonder at what he had experienced, the man began to speak of the miracle of the face he has seen reflected in the water. He spoke eloquently, beautifully, sorrowfully: "Today something happened to change my life. I saw a face that I knew must be mine, and yet it seems impossible. It was not the face of the terrible man who has lived here. I know what I have been, and yet my face tells of wondrous kindness. Now that I see what I really am, I am in anguish over what I have become. What can I do?" Deganawidah heard the passion and concern in the beautiful voice and invited the man to tell the story of how he had he come to be a cannibal.

With this encounter of the Peacemaker and the cannibal, we enter the realm of myth. Earlier parts of the Deganawidah story have been the stuff of legend, events that though unusual can be seen as having a basis in historical happenings. But with this episode, the legendary landscape has become an inscape, plummeting us into deeper, more universal territory. We are at a core moment that illumines one of the essential teachings this myth offers us: the need to see the True Face. Yet, as is generally the case in Native American stories, realization depends on enigma, subtlety, and looking at a situation with peripheral vision. A Navaho elder once told a visitor, "You must learn to look at the world twice. First, you must bring your eyes together in front so you can see each droplet of rain on the grass, so you can see the smoke rising from an anthill in the sunshine. Nothing should escape your notice. But you must learn to look again, with your eyes at the very edge of what is visible. Now you must see dimly if you wish to see things that are dim—visions, mist, and cloud people, animals which hurry past you in the dark. You must learn to look at the world twice if you wish to see all that there is to see." In this spirit, we might say, the True Face can only be seen in a second seeing, for it is watery, compounded of smoke and shadow as well as flesh and bone.

Second seeing can also illumine the details of a mythic story. Looked at with subtlety and peripheral vision, any detail of a myth can open up worlds of thought, conjecture, uneasiness, and ambiguity. If we pursue such details far enough, they will reconstellate at a place that can best be ascribed to race memory or what Carl Jung called the collective unconscious.

Using this criteria of second seeing, let us consider the issue of cannibalism. Worldwide, there has long been a massive dread and taboo against eating the flesh of another human. The taboo is so strong, the idea so repugnant, that some scholars speculate that at some time in the distant past, humans took part in wild celebrational events that ended in orgies of human flesh eating. These events created so profound a shock that its shadow lies permanently in the collective unconscious of the race. In *The Origins of the Sacred*, Dudley Young also suggests that the story of eating the apple in Genesis conceals the devouring of the dominant, "alpha" male for his spirit and power in a mad ecstasy of celebration and renewal— and ensuing guilt.[1] Young implies that this guilt and concerns that the cannibalistic act might recur caused emerging cultures to put strict boundaries around ritual group activity. So powerful is the taboo that some students of Judaism have argued that, as a Jew, Jesus could never have uttered the words that we use in Holy Communion: "This is my body, this is my blood; take and eat, take and drink in remembrance of me."

We must seek further for the origin of the Last Supper as it has been handed down to Christians. Other stories from the ancient past offer us tales of the annual sacrifice of the male who bears the sacred power, be he king or consort or shaman, who is done to death by a cruel upstart, a brother, or by the tribe in order to ensure that the crops will come again next year. The sacrificial mysteries of Osiris, Tammuz, Dionysus, or Orpheus all speak of this need to renew the earth with blood. These myths demonstrate that sharing the food of the body ritually is a way to participate in and to remember both the sacrifice and the love that engendered the god's willingness to be sacrificed. The central mystery of Christianity owes much to these ancient forebears. The Church bettered what it borrowed in the sacrament of the Mass, but did so while concealing and then forgetting the origins of the ritual in older and darker mysteries.

In other early societies, eating actual human flesh (not eucharistically transubstantiated) played its part in ritualized tribal warfare. Warriors the world over have cooked or eaten raw, in ceremonial action, the part of the body in which their enemy's strength was located: the arm, the leg, the heart, the brain. This action marks their ultimate triumph over the enemy and taking on the enemy's spiritual and physical power. In the years before the coming of Deganawidah, stories tell us that this practice had been corrupted into a deviant form of food gathering. The cannibal in our story had adopted a practice that all Native Americans viewed as the worst proof of social decay—killing and eating other humans as part of a normal diet. In fact, so profound is the Native understanding of the sanctity of life that eating any flesh must be accompanied by appropriate prayer and propitiation, so that the soul of the animal returns to Great Soul from whence it may come again to succor human life. Thus when Deganawidah journeyed to the cannibal, he moved toward the worst expression of the degeneracy of the society—a good man who, out of shock and sorrow, had fallen to inhuman behavior.

This is a good a place as any to confront the historic accounts of Iroquois cruelty. History, as we know, is written by the victors, and the Iroquois were not ultimately triumphant, although they are still present and unforgettable. Their present-day leaders offer guidance and hope to many who seek the ways of the Peacemaker across the world. But for at least two hundred years the Iroquois epitomized for both surrounding tribes and white settlers a stance of unflinching opposition. They bore the stigma of such opposition even in the name by which we know them, a name given by their enemies: *Iroquois* means Terrifying Man in the Algonquian tongue.

However, there are also numerous accounts of the Iroquois going forth in peace, carrying the Great Law of Deganawidah, and being met and slaughtered by the French, for example, who thought they were weaklings for being willing to listen to all sides of a story (as Deganawidah had taught them). At the same time, there are accounts of the terrors of Iroquois' successes in battle. They "come like foxes . . . attack like lions, take flight like birds," as one writer described them. However, historians have pointed out that until the whites came, much of Iroquois warfare was ceremonial, consisting of commandolike raids for goods and status. But when the Iroquois understood the deadliness of their white adversaries and the method of "divide and conquer" which the Colonists were using to defeat the Native peoples, Iroquois ferocity grew—as did accounts of their cruelty.

Eyewitness accounts by French Jesuits, for example, describe both what befell prisoners of war captured by the Iroquois and the similar fate of Iroquois folk taken by Hurons and Algonquins. Women and children were almost always adopted into the clan that defeated them. Males, however, were dragged across country from the field of battle tied to a bark carrier, a kind of wheelbarrow without wheels, by leather shackles called slave bands. Once a male prisoner reached the settlement, he was forced to run a gauntlet of those who had lost members of their family to his tribe. If he endured this bravely, he had the chance of being adopted by the clan mother who had most recently lost a child. (In fact, Seneca records report that at one time there were more male adoptees in their tribe than men born into it.) But if the mothers declared themselves still too bitter and angry at the prisoner's tribe, they could decree his death. The condemned man was feasted, sung to, and then tortured to death, mercilessly, ritualistically, and slowly. For his part, the prisoner was asked to play his role gallantly and to sing songs that told his own story, celebrated his totem allies, and taunted his persecutors. Sometimes pieces of his flesh were cut away from his body while he was still alive, then roasted and eaten by the observers. Here ingesting the meat that held such bravery was a way of honoring the dying man's courage.

We must remember, however, that accounts such as these do not reflect the word that Deganawidah brought any more than the Inquisition reflected the words of Jesus, or the common practice of drawing and quartering prisoners as a spectator sport reflected the highest levels of thought and accomplishment of the English Renaissance. The lesson seems to be that if we are to embrace the New Mind, we must, like the cannibal, look fearlessly without denial at what we have been and, perhaps, to some extent, still are. By his very presence, Deganawidah brought about a turning of the times, a transforming of shadows of Iroquois culture and consciousness. His vision turned the ordinary pathology of the culture into extraordinary promise and new life. Thus a man who had made it his business to kill and devour other humans saw a True Face in the water of his cooking pot. Notice that his revelation did not focus on the ugliness and horror of his past actions, but rather on the beauty of essence—his ideal and Higher Self. When the cannibal saw the glory of human essence, he became conscious and his actions were transformed. So might we all.

Just as cannibalism can be seen as a many-faceted symbol when it is looked at with second sight, so too can other details in this episode of the Deganawidah story be teased into revealing deeper secrets. The mirror is another such potent symbol. Many studies have pointed to the mirror as essential to awakening consciousness. As myths and stories the world over attest, the ability to see our reflected selves seems a requisite to awareness and maturation.

In *Iron John*, Robert Bly offers a marvelous disquisition on the face that stares back at us from the mirror. He writes:

> When we look into our own eyes in the mirror . . . we have the inescapable impression, so powerful and astonishing, that someone is looking back at us . . . That experience of being looked back at sobers us up immediately . . . Someone looks back questioning, serious, alert, and without intent to comfort; and we feel more depth in the eyes looking at us than we ordinarily sense in our own eyes as we stare out at the world. How strange! Who could it be that is looking at us? We conclude that it is another part of us, the half that we don't allow to pass out of our eyes when we glance at others—and that darker and more serious half looks back at us only at rare times.[2]

It is a fascinating fact of cultural history that the use of the mirror seems to run parallel to the development of consciousness itself. Periods of growing awareness of the self seem always to be accompanied by remarkable increases in the use, distribution, and manufacture of mirrors. People in antiquity, especially in Egypt, ancient China, and Greece, made use of strongly reflecting surfaces, but long contemplation of one's own face was considered aberrant behavior. The mirror as a thing of constant use arose only in the Renaissance. As Morris Berman has shown in his wonderful book

Coming to Our Senses, the rise of mirrors in the late Renaissance suggests "the emergence of an increasing psychic distance between human beings, and within human beings. Self/Other unity begins to break down . . . and mirror manufacture parallels this psychic development. Nation-states, armies, self-portraits, perspective, the collapse of magic—all of these represent an increasing preoccupation with boundaries, with sharp Self/Other distinctions, and the interest in the mirror is really an icon of the whole process."[3] In medieval times, by way of contrast, mirrors were not much used. The psychology of relationship was entirely different; people were much more spontaneous and immersed in each other.

By the seventeenth century, the use of mirrors had virtually become a fetish, with the height of the obsession being the famous Hall of Mirrors in Versailles, in which the courtiers of Louis XIV, *Le Roi Soleil*, could regard themselves and each other constantly from every possible angle. And as might be expected, with the growth of the ego and of acute self-consciousness in the last several centuries comes an exponential increase in the use of mirrors, until today they are so ubiquitous that they are virtually prosthetic extensions of ourselves. Does this development signal that we are moving to another rung in the evolution of the individuating psychic process? Or are we lost in a temporary (we hope) byway of obsession with looks and narcissism?

Looked at in this light, the mirror-mediated encounter between Deganawidah and the cannibal suggests several interpretations. It is a delicious irony that the cannibal is only able to face what he has been when he sees the face of another and "mistakes" it for his own. Thus, it seems, the mirror not only reflects the ordinary self but also draws us beyond the everyday level to a view of the Watcher, the High Self, the archetypal One who is really sponsoring us, the One whose True Face reflects our essence.

Moreover, the mirror episode of the Deganawidah story gives us entrance into one of the most intriguing pieces of Iroquois culture, the concept of the False Face. Iroquois storytellers speak of Sky Woman, who, in the origins of time, was tricked by her husband into falling from heaven through the uprooted Tree of Light into the earth realm. She landed on turtle's back and, shortly thereafter, gave birth to a daughter, who herself bore twin spirits, one good and one evil. The daughter died when the Evil Spirit burst forth from her side. Since then, the world has known contention between Great Spirit and Evil Spirit.

From the mother's body, Great Spirit created the sun and moon and stars, and added rivers, mountains, valleys, seas, and all living things. But Evil Spirit was also busy, creating war and divisiveness. The two fought a huge battle and, after days of conflict, Great Spirit won and banished Evil Spirit. But Evil Spirit still had allies around to make life difficult for the people of the world. The original False Face was one of the evil twin's progeny. He set his might against Great Spirit by creating illness and, for his actions, was condemned to spend eternity healing the sick. The False Face Society of the Iroquois, a group of healers who wore masks of the False Face, surely has its origins in this story. Any person healed by the False Face Society became a member of the society.

The roles of the Great Spirit and Evil Spirit are played here by Deganawidah and the cannibal, the True Face and the False. With the coming of Deganawidah, a new dispensation was at hand, and the cannibal, instead of being banished, was shown his true being and spent the rest of his life as a healer who brought the Good News of life and peace to replace death and suffering. Having been healed of his cannibalism through seeing the True Face, the man became Deganawidah's primary ally and friend. As we will see, this friendship became the model for leadership among the Iroquois, each clan being governed by a primary leader and his partner.

The overarching mythic element of this part of the story, however, is the stance and actions of the archetypal Peacemaker. To be a Peacemaker is to be willing to encounter the worst of us, our shadow selves, our most fearsome nature. Here, too, the details of the story contain potent teachings. As the Peacemaker, Deganawidah does not confront the cannibal directly, but rather by climbing the roof and looking down through smoke into a cauldron of life and death. By looking into the kettle at the corpse, in some sense, Deganawidah

enters the dead man's body and the fire, for the cannibal's sake—
and for ours. When we, in our desolation, look into the cauldron
of our inner self, too often we expect to see only the things we
have killed or lost or devoured. Deganawidah teaches us that we
can learn to see instead the face of the archetypal bringer of peace,
a harbinger of the Good News of who we really are and what we
can do about it.

When we ask how it happens that the cannibal failed to look
up, or to see some mixture of his own face mingled with Deganawidah's, or how it is that he did not recognize the face when he
saw Deganawidah standing before his house, we ask questions that
can be answered psychologically, but which lack the relevance or
power of the mythic point of view. Absorbed in our day-to-day life,
we, too, often fail to look up. But when by providential chance we
finally do see something that speaks to our essence, a fundamental
change takes place within us, and nothing we see thereafter is the
same. Seeing a face in water or in smoke is different from seeing
it in the flesh; seeing reflected truth is often far more potent than
seeing it directly. Knowing now the absolute beauty of his essential being, the former cannibal will expect to see absolute beauty
everywhere.

When the cannibal tells his story to Deganawidah, we are again
in the realm of myth. The story is slippery; it buckles back and
forth upon itself like a giant snake, for in it we first meet the great
antagonist of Deganawidah's life, the sorcerer Tadodaho. Here again
is the mythic encounter between the good and evil twins. There are
many versions of this part of the myth. Here is one:

The man who became the cannibal had been known as an orator,
a man who spoke eloquently in the style and tradition of Native
American peoples. He had lived among the Onondaga tribe, where
there also lived a terrible sorcerer. The orator, a man of goodness and
noble character, kept trying to persuade the sorcerer, whose name
was Tadodaho, or Atoroho in some other traditions, to give up his
evil ways. In addition to sorcery, Tadodaho was also a cannibal.
As a result of his opposition to Tadodaho, the orator's family had

sorcery inflicted on it, and his wife and four of his seven daughters had died. Whereupon the orator had become so filled with agony that he went mad and took on the very character of the sorcerer, saying, "I will outdo him in all his evil." So saying, the orator lost his true self and became a cannibal, living alone in the forest. But now this great persuader, this great orator, had looked into the kettle and had seen his Deep Face, his True Face. Because he had once been a great and good man himself and had committed such terrible wrong, his misery was enormous. He had been reminded by the face he saw of who and what he really was.

Deganawidah listened to the story and replied, "That is a wonderful story! You see what you have just done. You have shifted a basic pattern of vengeful response in your life, and nothing is more difficult than breaking patterns set so deep within us. Congratulations! A new kind of awareness, a New Mind, if you will, has been born in you today, a desire to see justice done, to restore health and sanity and, through this, a recognition of your path to spiritual power."

How vital it is that we tell our stories, even our most dangerous-seeming secrets, to someone who carries the Mind of the Maker. That is how we can see our deep truth mirrored, reflected back to us in ways which authenticate our experience while inviting us to enter upon our true life's purpose. If only we can learn to listen as Deganawidah listened and to respond as he responded!

"But wait," the former cannibal wailed. "How can this be? All I feel is agony over my past."

Deganawidah answered him kindly. "Yes, agony, because the quality of your New Mind cannot bear to remember things done in blind ignorance. But do not shut down or cause those memories to go underground. Look at the truth about yourself, but know that there is a deeper truth and that it is possible for us to heal our past by working for peace and justice in the present. We can approach the people we have harmed and this time offer them solace and a healing."

"What can I do?"

"I have listened to you speak. You are a fine speaker, with a beautiful and persuasive power to your voice. My message requires just such a gift. As you hear, I cannot speak without stuttering. I ask you to work with me. Together we can carry the Good News of peace and power to all people who can hear us."

The former cannibal's reply followed the traditional formula. "Your message is a good one. I take hold of it. I embrace it. How shall we begin?"

Deganawidah said, "It is important first for us to share a meal. I will go into the forest and find appropriate food for us to eat. While I do that, will you go get some fresh water to use for cooking?"

Deganawidah cautioned his new friend about the importance of dipping his pail into the brook as it runs downstream and, thus, not trying to work against the forces of nature. This illustrates the importance of using the whole mind to discern when we are moving against the currents of habituated thought and outmoded ways of being, in other words, against the natural flow of the universe. When we do not try to fight nature, but instead align ourselves with its rhythms, we restore our spirit and energy and are able to fight those things which authentically should be battled.

When he came out of the forest, Deganawidah was carrying a deer with large antlers. This was food the Holder of Heavens had ordained as appropriate for humans where there were no vegetables (or women to plant them) and also on those occasions that called for ceremonial feasting. The antlers of the deer were blessed by Deganawidah and decreed as a symbol of leadership to be worn in the coming time of peace.

Deer Power is a common theme in those places on earth where the deer forages. Prince Rama of India sought the Golden Deer; Hercules chased and captured a female deer with golden horns; the Buddha became a deer in one of his incarnations in order to save others. Early English mummer's plays used deer antlers as the totemic symbol of Christ, and the antlers recur in Shakespeare's forest plays with mystical overtones. Among many Native peoples the deer mask, the calling of the deer for the hunt, and the deer dance are sacred events. Perhaps when one wears the headdress of deer antlers, as do the chiefs of the Iroquois, one takes on the ability of the animal to move swiftly and gracefully through thick, dim woods of thought and responsibility. Perhaps, too, we see in this tradition not only the power of the animal, but also the belief that as the deer is willing to serve humans, so a great chief must be willing to serve his people, even sacrifice himself should the need arise. Even today members of the Iroquois nation study the meaning of deer antlers, as well as all other aspects of the law, proclaiming truthfully, as scholars of sacred texts always do, that there is no end to the enlightenment possible through such study.

Deganawidah's new ally now wished to know what name the peace age would have. In the Iroquois language, the words for the New Time are *Kanonsionni,* which means Longhouse or League or Confederacy, and *Kayanerenhkowa,* meaning the Great Law or the Great Peace. Again, as with Jigonhsasee, the Peacemaker told his new convert of his vision of the way people would live in peace in the community of the Longhouse, because they would share under- standing of the one law.

Since his new friend was eager to begin his service, Deganawidah gave him his first assignment. As might be expected, it was the most difficult task possible, physically and emotionally. With his New Mind, his new fearlessness, and so much pain to assuage, Degana- widah directed him to go first to the evil wizard of the Onondagas, Tadodaho, who killed without mercy and devoured what he killed.

In dismay, the other replied, "But that's the man who caused me to go mad and become a cannibal!"

"Yes," Deganawidah replied, "and that is why he is the person you have to go to."

"Do you know what he's like?" Deganawidah's new friend asked. "He has a body with seven crooks in it. He has a club for his fist. He has a snake for a penis, which is wrapped around his body, and snakes for his matted hair. His evil power is enormous."

Deganawidah replied, "Yes, and that is why the cause of peace cannot go further without his becoming peaceful. Go to him again— again and again, if necessary. Go to him with the message of peace. Of course, he will drive you away, over and over again. Expect that. But at last you will prevail. For this purpose, I will give you a new name. From this moment on you shall be Hiawatha, which means He Who Combs, for you shall comb the snakes out of Tadodaho's hair."

This powerful story speaks volumes to the twentieth century. A principle disease of modern times is the horror of our own face. Survivalists, ecologists, ethnologists, and psychologists alike, aided and abetted by the media, too often and with glee excoriate and condemn the human species, filling us with dread about our own nature. The psychological climate hasn't changed much since John Calvin and John Knox thundered at us about hopelessly inherent human evil. Unfortunately, the events of the twentieth century would seem to confirm this diagnosis, for what is this century but a terrible cycle of wounding followed by devourment followed by wounding followed by devourment, a century of mythic proportions in terms of the violence given and received?

This awful pattern is true for individuals as well as for nations. Never before have so many people been so wounded psychologically as in our times. Or, in the language of this story, never before have so many people been so much in need of seeing and being seen in terms of their Deeper Face. For above and beyond all this wounding, there on the roof, looking through the smoke hole of our personal and collective psyche, is another face—the Deeper Face of the twentieth century, the story and the face of the higher being, the Peacemaker in us. It asks to be seen, to be acknowledged, and with it, a Deeper Story that is trying to emerge. Until this happens, the current cycle of wounding and devouring will continue until there is no one and nothing left to be seen. Like the cannibal, we are haunted by the question of what we can do to get beyond this cycle. This is the question that the story of the Peacemaker tries to answer. In what follows we will discover some of the ways in which this can be done.

NOTES

[1] Dudley Young, *Origins of the Sacred: The Ecstasies of Love and War* (New York: Harper Perennial, 1992), pp. 157–159.

2 Robert Bly, *Iron John* (Reading, Mass.: Addison-Wesley, 1990), p. 85.

3 Morris Berman, *Coming To Our Senses* (New York: Bantam, 1991), p. 49.

SEEING THE DEEP FACE

TIME: One hour.

MATERIALS: For those going solo, a mirror is absolutely necessary.

MUSIC: Native American flute music.

INSTRUCTIONS FOR GOING SOLO: Again, this is a process best done with one other person. If that is not possible, then tape the instructions and look with fresh eyes at your own face in a mirror. You could even recite a mythic incantation, saying with closed eyes: "Mirror, mirror, on the wall, who and what is in this face on the sensory level?" Then opening your eyes, describe out loud what you see on the sensory level. Repeat the same process for the other levels.

In this process we will be playing Deganawidah and Hiawatha at the moment when Hiawatha sees his own Deep Face in the face of Deganawidah reflected in the kettle. This means we will be seeing another person in ways that are deeper than the incrustations of habit or conditioning. To see another deeply, as if for the first time, is to enter into knowledge of his or her essence and, perhaps, to release something of this essence to the person seen. Too often we get lazy in our perceptions of other people, especially those who are most familiar to us. We take them for granted, not allowing for their uniqueness or the fullness of what they are and what they yearn to be. We project certain static qualities upon them; as a result, they frequently find themselves trapped in our perceptions, responding only in the ways we expect them to. When we make the effort to see them afresh, we give them one of the greatest gifts that one human being can give to another—the gift of deep seeing.

My studies into the domains of consciousness point to at least four major levels of the human psyche. I've termed these the *sensory/physical*, the *psychological/historical*, the *mythic/symbolic*, and *spiritual/integrative*. Each of these levels evokes a different style of imagery and reflection. In the following exercise we will discover the characteristic imagery of each level as well as how to use the levels to deepen our understanding and appreciation of the fullness of the other, and of ourselves.

SCRIPT FOR THE GUIDE:
Begin by walking around until you see someone who you think looks something like you. The resemblance doesn't have to be physical. Men and women can choose each other. Just wander around until you find somebody who you think either looks somewhat like you or with whom there is a sense of resonance or familiarity. When you get a match, sit down together so that you are facing each other.

In this part of the process, you will be describing to your partner what you see as you look at his or her face on a purely sensory level. But the seeing is a Deep Seeing, so you won't necessarily see and describe brown hair or gray hair, a square face or round face. Your seeing will be much broader and deeper with images drawn, perhaps, from the sensory and physical worlds of nature or the descriptions of landscapes or environments. You will cast wide to find the metaphors to describe your seeing. Let me offer an example of sensory level seeing from the process as it happened at Mystery School.

Partner A (looking at Partner B): I see blue eyes with a great lake of blue on the outside of the iris, and then a kind of ice, beautiful flecks of ice blue, on an inner circle of the iris, and then the pool of the pupil that's filled with both blackness and light. And I see your mouth as a rose, and the upper lip flowering a little fuller than the lower. And this rose is growing on a strong but feminine cliff that is also a very firm chin. A rounded square. Squaring the circle.

Partner B (looking at Partner A): And I see eyebrows that are eagle's wings soaring over caverns that hold the treasures of ancient knowings. Many different paths lead out and away from these caverns and travel into a forest of many plants and trees. Ah, you smiled, and suddenly in the midst of this landscape, all these shiny piano keys just showed up. . . .

What you are offering to each other as you gaze at your partner's face is not just description. It is a Deep Seeing, a novel seeing, as if you are seeing a rare and wondrous being who rises out of the water to visit you or a new, incredible landscape come upon for the first time.

To begin, just shift your body a little bit and breathe deeply. Open your eyes very wide and then squeeze them shut. Open, squeeze. Open, squeeze. Now have a sense of breathing into the eyes . . . and then let it all go. Once more, breathe into the eyes . . . and let it all go. Continue to do this and, as you do, let all your expectations go. Let everything go, especially your usual habits of seeing. Your seeing is becoming new. You will see as if on the first day of creation. Breathe into your eyes . . . and let go . . . Breathe into your eyes . . . and let go.

And now, if you would, have the sense that you're looking into water, so that the face of your partner is coming up out of water. And you see the most remarkable face emerging through the cool and clear water. Speak now to your partner describing to them what you see on a sensory level in their face. First one speak, and then the other. You have five minutes of clock time to do this, but it will be equal to all the time you need. (Five minutes.)

Come to a natural ending now, realizing that you will continue, because each level feeds the next.

The next level is the psychological or historical. What you'll be seeing and expressing here are psychological or biographical patterns that may or may not relate to the person's experience. These may be traits of character or personality, like strength, forbearance, irony, melancholy, whimsy, humor. They may be events from the person's life, or even events from the lives of his or her ancestors. Regardless of what you may already know about your partner, you should speak only about what you're seeing. Let me read you an example of seeing at this level from the process as it took place at Mystery School.

Partner A: Well, in those blue eyes, where the center part that's around the dark pool of the pupil is, I see Nordic people who understand both the blue of the sky and the blue of ice. I see a kind of poignant understanding in those eyes and reflected in the face. And I'm seeing the shadow and the light and an appreciation of shadow and light. I see a stoicism, a capacity to "hold the line," and a steadfastness that's there in the way the mouth is shaped and the way you're holding it. A determination too, so that you can take hold of things—it feels like the teeth have taken hold of something and the mouth is holding it fast.

Partner B: I'm seeing history here. I see a hearty woman of Elizabethan times, the kind of strapping woman who runs a large household and farm, brews her own ale, partners her husband, who is the bailiff of the shire, and offers her barn to the traveling players to perform in. I see also a merry maverick, a woman who has had a wonderful time exploring the many alternate paths of life and has come home full of rich living.

Now taking turns, speak to each other about what you see on a psychological and/or historical plane. Whatever you do, don't offer therapy. Just describe as richly as you can what you see. You have five minutes of clock time to do this for each other. (Five minutes.)

Come to a natural ending now, and let us prepare to move to an even deeper level of seeing.

Would you shake your body all over a bit, rub your hands, and rub your face. Now close and open your eyes, and continue to close and open them, close and open, close and open. . . . And shift. Actually feel your body shift to a another level. We're going to descend into an even deeper level of the psyche, down to the level of myth and story and symbol.

And again, let arise the sense of water, so that when you're seeing the face, you're seeing through water. And remember that what you see may not be at all what the person is really like. It's just what you see. And now as you look deeply at the face you see through the water, you find yourself in the realm of story and myth, where the person's local story becomes part of a much Larger Story, where the local person is part of Great Person. In this realm, we are not our bounded historical selves; we are the Hero or Heroine with a Thousand, a Million Faces. Our story is Great Story. We are mythic, and we are part of dimensions that are both real and superreal.

There is great art and poetry in the knowings of this level, and within each of us is the tale that transcends all local histories and conditions. It is the tale of the person at the edge of reality. It is the tale of Christ; it is the tale of the Buddha; it is the tale of Saint Joan, or of Oedipus, or of Persephone. The Deep Face is that of Spider Woman, Corn Mother, Coyote, the Trickster, Deganawidah. It is the face of an archetype, a legendary or mythic figure who inhabits the local face and soul, a god or goddess perhaps, a principle of living. Let me read you an example of seeing at this level from the process as it unfolded at Mystery School.

Participant: I see a very playful Sophia. I see someone who, in addition to all the sorrows that that goddess came into life to embody and to experience, is a Sophia who loves life lustily and devours experience. I'm seeing the Warrior Woman, a powerful and vibrant Amazon Woman. And partly because you have your head tilted like that and because of your hair, I'm seeing that you are also the Feathered Serpent, the one who lifts off the earth and, with wide open eyes and feathers, dances the skies.

Now, taking turns, describe to your partner what you see in his or her face on a mythic and symbolic level. You have five minutes of clock time to complete this part of the process. (Five minutes.)

Come please to a natural ending.

We will be moving now to the most profound level of seeing. Please stretch now, and as you stretch, I'm going to ask you to find yourself entering the deepest level of seeing—the spiritual level. At this level you begin to see the True Face behind all the other faces— the spiritual essence of the other. Here resides the divine portion that inhabits each person; here is seen that beingness of love that moves the sun and all the stars. Here is seen that part of the other that is immortal and eternal, that knows all things, is present in all times and places. Here the story seen is the Spirit story. Here is seen the source place, the true home, the world beyond tomorrow or yesterday. Let me read you an example of such seeing from Mystery School.

Participant: I see that the cloud of hair at the top of your head opens into a spill of light that surrounds your whole being and that sources the light above, rather than the other way around. Yes, it's feeding the light, the general light of the world. And in the blue eyes I see the flight through the sky, through the lakes, through the cold of outer space. The coolness of color, and yet the black heat in the middle of the Spirit moving. . . .

Now, open and close your eyes several times and, trusting yourself to see, look into the wondrous face before you from the level of pure Spirit. Take turns describing what you see. You have five minutes of clock time. (Five minutes.)

Come now to a natural ending.

Now, continuing to sit with your partner, looking deeply at each other, ask yourself, is what I have been describing about the other really me? Is what I have been describing in some way my own Deeper Face? You don't have to discuss the answer, although you may do so, if you wish. . . .(One minute.)

Now what I'm going to ask you to do is to reach out—first one and then the other, or together—and take hold of the Deep Face reflected in the face of your partner. As you hold that face between your hands, receive the essence of all that it has come to mean: landscapes and emotions, stories and Spirit. Take the essence of that

True Face into yourself—leaving it as part of the other as well—so that you have more of the awareness and the conscious knowing of your own True Face. . . .

Speak now the words of deep acceptance, the same words spoken in Deganawidah and Hiawatha's day: "I take hold of it. I embrace it. I take hold of it. I embrace it." Know, as Hiawatha did, that the Noble Being you saw is yourself. And feel from this the change, the deepening, the taking in of the possibility of doing deeper work in the world—the Good Work, the New Mind that comes with the Deeper Face. And receive that, oh so deeply! And then bow, or make some gesture of rich acknowledgment to your partner. . . .

And then would you wander through the room, please, looking at each other, because I want you to see all the New Minds and New Faces that are in this room.

5

FALL INTO THE NEW FORM

In many classic archetypal tales, the hero is eager to confront the forces of evil. In this story, too, we find the Peacemaker willing to face the sorcerer himself first, to prepare the way for Hiawatha's visit.

"You are invited to open your mind to new possibilities of peace," Deganawidah told the snarling sorcerer. "No more war. No more killing. No more sorcery."

The evil one, his head spiky with snakes, replied to Deganawidah's quiet invitation with a great howling cry, "*HWE-DO-NE-E-E-E-EH?*" ("When will this be?") According to one of my Iroquois friends, the sorcerer's cry was the Onondaga equivalent of "over my dead body."

Undeterred, Deganawidah continued on his journey eastward, moving toward the rising sun. In each village, he presented his message of peace to the desperate people, thus fulfilling the promise he made to the hunters he met when he first arrived on the southern shores of the Great Beautiful Lake. The cycle of wounding and devourment—of cannibalism as the destruction of one tribe by the other, of killing and revenge leading to still more killing—had created a state of perpetual war between the tribes. But Deganawidah, being tribeless, was considered neutral and could transcend village kinship loyalties, as well as the cycle of revenge killings. He was the ultimate outcast among his own people, the Hurons, because he was born without a father and without acceptance, and among the other tribes, because he was an outsider with no ties of kinship. Having no ties, he had the potential to create a nation that transcended, yet built upon, tribal structures, weaving individual tribes into a larger confederacy and making use of the Longhouse as the image for the greater Longhouse of the nations. Because he had no personal history with these tribes, he could openly voice a dissident opinion and act as a messenger of peace without disgrace or accusations of cowardice.

This description of the hero as one who is unpatterned, unpatroned, and unparented relates Deganawidah to many other mythical figures. "The son of the widow woman" looms large in the lore of those who take the hero's journey and bring in their wake the changing of the ways of the world. Contemplative and dreamy, these heroes are liminal men who find their missing parent in the depths. One thinks, for example, of Horus in the Egyptian myths, conceived of Isis by her dead husband Osiris and raised almost exclusively by women. Not until adolescence is he visited by Osiris in a dream and given further training for his role in life. Parsifal, the hero of many of the medieval Grail stories, is also half-parented, his father having died when he was a baby. He is raised in the deep forest by his mother, who tries to keep him innocent of war, sex, and the ways of men. Since he knows nothing of male culture and patterning, he is free to make up his life as he goes along. He has no boundaries as to what is proper or probable in behavior or profession. Free of strictures and the "hard facts" of reality, he can do impossible things. Like Parsifal, Deganawidah had no preconceived notions and no cultural expectations; living in the open moment and traveling the open road, he too was able to redeem a wasteland world.

As he traveled, Deganawidah visited the Mohawks first, who were known as "the people who possess the flint." Mohawk warriors, devastated by wars, were suspicious in the extreme, regarding any wanderer as a potential enemy. So Deganawidah did not enter the Mohawk settlement. Instead, he smoked his pipe outside the village near the edge of the forest. A passerby approached Deganawidah and asked him who he was.

"My name is Deganawidah," he replied. "The Great Creator who has given life to all of us has given me the task of creating peace among you."

"You've got your work cut out for you in this place," said the war-weary man. "But you're an interesting one, especially with that stutter. Come with me. Let us go to the settlement, and you can present your thoughts about peace to my people."

Notice that the fact that Deganawidah spoke so poorly made everybody listen with special attention. The natural tendency when we hear someone with a stutter is to repeat what we thought we heard.

"What was that word, please?"

"R-r-righteousn-n-ess."

"Oh, righteousness. And you are saying it can bring about what?"

In this way Deganawidah's handicap actually worked to his advantage. One could make fun of or laugh at an earnest speaker stuttering over ideas of a great peace, but one would not feel threatened. Such a speaker's open-hearted vulnerability would give him and his message great spiritual force. What is more, the listeners would have to get involved in an immediate dialogue over the ideas in order simply to understand them.

"P-p-peace will c-c-c-ome with the New M-m-mind. . ."

"I know what he's trying to say. He's for our giving up . . ."

"Be quiet, and let him speak."

"I b-b-bring the New M-m-mind to each one of y-y-ou."

Hearing Deganawidah's message, the Mohawk people were much taken by the idea of the Good News, a New Mind, a High Peace, and a Longhouse of extended community. Their situation was much like the open moment in which we find ourselves today. After a century of devastating wars, genocide, holocausts, and the breakdown of the immune systems of both the individual body and the body politic, many people today are saying, "What would it be like to have a planetary society? What would it be like to live in the ultimate Longhouse, a world in which cultures are encouraged and empowered and, at the same time, linked in a multicultural, planetary entity?"

As is the case with many contemporary movements dedicated to these goals, the Mohawk people were very encouraged by this notion. The chiefs, however, were suspicious, as we might imagine some world political leaders would be today. One can almost hear their grumbling, "Troublemaker. Huron spy. Who is he to tell us what to do? We've been leading these people for years. We know what do. This fellow can barely talk, and he's trying to give us new laws?" In these words of fear and denial, we can almost hear the old warriors in China, in the Pentagon, in the Presidium in Russia, responding to younger people who hold a vision of renewal and reform.

The chiefs told Deganawidah that the tribes to the east and west of the Mohawk settlements with whom they were always at war would never agree to his grand scheme. "It's not us. It's not us," they cried. "*We* could do it. They will never agree! How could we dare to begin such a thing when our neighbors continue to invade us?"

To be the first to lay down arms and announce a policy of peace is a troubling act, especially in a world rife with justified paranoia, and most especially if you are responsible for the safety and welfare of a nation. To counter this, Deganawidah created a field of belief by telling everyone he met for years on end, "I bring news of the Great Peace." In this way, the preliminary vibration of the new possibility was spread through the land, beginning with the hunters, who were asked to bring the message to their settlements, and with Jigonhsasee, whose lodge became a place where warriors could hear of the new peace.

What is more, Deganawidah walked his talk. Through peaceful words and ways he had changed the life of a dangerous cannibal and had dared to venture into places haunted by the most evil of men. He would perform other acts of courage as well to prove that his message was true. One could assume that he was either a complete fool and madman or that there was something to him. Like Parsifal, whose name means both "piercer of the vale" and "holy fool," Deganawidah was both holy fool and bringer of a new dispensation. The new field of belief created by his actions and words changed the habits of centuries of warfare and increased the options for Indian society.

Deganawidah's method is vitally important because it suggests a strategy for change applicable to many situations. When an action changes the form and pattern of habitual behavior in one area, it facilitates and encourages similar changes in the future and in other areas. This model has been most recently confirmed by the thinking of English botanist and theorist Rupert Sheldrake. Sheldrake has presented impressive evidence pointing to the possibility that the habits and laws of nature are not static but can change their forms and functions through new discoveries and the adaptation of new habits. Sheldrake theorizes the existence of what he calls "morphogenetic fields," invisible organized fields weaving across time and space (and within which we are all connected), which act as blueprints for new structures. Seeding the morphogenetic field with new forms and behaviors adds to the species "memory" from which all organisms can then draw. This means that once a substance, an individual, or even a society learns a new behavior, the causative, morphogenetic field of that entity is changed, and the next substance, individual, or society learns the new behavior much more quickly. According to Sheldrake, the more an event is duplicated, the more powerful its morphogenetic field becomes. Thus people in the twentieth century learn to operate machinery and ride bicycles much more quickly that people did in the previous century. Similarly, children tend to learn to operate computers faster than their parents. So, by affirming constantly the truth of his message, Deganawidah changed the prevailing field of war into a field of peace. For hundreds of years thereafter, it would appear that the Iroquois lived in one of the most remarkably successful and peaceful societies the world has ever known. Moreover, many historians have argued, and we must agree, that Deganawidah was instrumental in establishing the field in which both the American commonwealth and similar democracies the world over could grow and flourish.

And so, Deganawidah insisted to the doubting chiefs, the holders of the old morphogenetic field, "The Great Peace will come when all of you embrace the New Law."

"We would like to believe you," the chiefs replied, "but your idea is so outlandish that we need something to prove its truth to us. We need a sign. We need some act on your part that will demonstrate that you are not a Huron agent come to divide and destroy us, to make us weak and peaceful, so that your warriors can sack us."

Looking out over the landscape, one of the chiefs pointed to a tree nearby, a deformed and twisted oak, which grew over the edge of a waterfall. "If your words are true," they challenged, "climb into the tree that leans over the falls. We will cut the tree down, and you will fall with it a long, long, long way. If you are still alive in the morning, we will become part of the Great Peace."

And so Deganawidah climbed into the ancient oak, and the people begin chopping at the tree with their hatchets. After a while, Deganawidah himself wrapped his legs around a branch, leaned down, and begin to help to hack down the tree with his own hatchet. As he did this, a strong rain began to fall. The Mohawks stood back amazed as Deganawidah attacked with a savage fury the tree which he himself named as the Tree of War.

I enjoy Ken Carey's vision of what happened next. In his rendering of the story in *The Return of the Bird Tribes*, he has Deganawidah say, "It is I who have said that the twisted Tree of War must be cut from your lives. It is I who will cut away this tree and fall with it into the gorge. My act will give you a teaching that my words have not. No man should ever be afraid to cut falsehood from his life, even if it is the very thing upon which he is standing. Once he recognizes it, he should not fear to let it fall away. For to remain standing upon a lie, once it is known to be false, is to destroy your own future peace and joy. And there is no value to living if such as these are your roots."[1]

When only a few more hacks with the hatchet were needed to fell the tree completely, Deganawidah stood in the branches and looked down at the now respectful faces of the Mohawks. The rain had ceased falling, and an extraordinary rainbow arched across the sky. Deganawidah pointed to the sun and spoke of the many circles— the sacred hoops in nature, the cycling of the sun and the moon, the cycling of the seasons, the circles of our lives, and the sacred hoop of the tribe that could be, as well, part of the Sacred Hoop of the Nations. Then he pointed to the rainbow which appeared as a half-circle, and he said, "Each tribe is like one of the colors you see before you that compose the rainbow. Do you see where the colors touch and intermingle? This is the trade between tribes that live in peace. Where people honor the ways of the Great Spirit, new and more beautiful colors come into being. Through their exchange, there is plenty for all. The rainbow has been given to us as a sign to remind us that we must become tribes living in harmony together on the earth. The rainbow is a half-circle that we must complete in our hearts. Except for self-defense, there is no place for violence in a heart that honors the teaching of the Great Spirit. Remove such error from your lives as I now remove this tree from its false roots."[2]

With that, Deganawidah leaped up higher into the tree and landed as hard as he could on the branch which arched over the cliff. With a mighty crack, the twisted oak split. Some say that the tree was uprooted absolutely and Deganawidah with it. Holding onto the branch, Deganawidah and the tree fell end over end over end, the long, long way down to the ground. As he was falling, clinging to the branches, Deganawidah knew that whether he lived or died, the point had been made to the Mohawks and that they would be more peaceable after what they had seen.

It was an absurd thing to do. Deganawidah was willing to risk everything to carry his message home. Evidently, his fall was broken by a succession of branches. Deganawidah himself said later that it was as if the Great Spirit had put up branches to help him. He landed with only a few scratches and bruises. In one version of the story, he picked himself up and went off into the forest to catch a buck, arriving back at the Mohawk camp carrying the venison on his back as a gift. In another version, the Mohawks went to look for Deganawidah the next morning because they could not see him after the fall. They found smoke coming up from an abandoned shelter and Deganawidah there smoking his pipe.

In either case, the Mohawks held a great feast for Deganawidah and dropped further resistance to his ideas. According to the oral tradition of the Iroquois, the Chief Warrior spoke for all when he said, "Yesterday, I was in great doubt, for words, however good, do not always betoken the thing that is. Now I am in doubt no longer. This is a great man, who reveals to us the Mind of the Maker of Life. Let us accept his message. Let us take hold of the Good News of peace and power."[3]

Deganawidah responded, "The day is early and young and so is the New Mind young and tender. And as the new sun rises and proceeds surely on its course in the sky, so also shall the Young Mind prevail and prosper among humans. There shall be peace. Your children and your grandchildren and your descendents to the seventh generation—those whose faces are yet beneath the ground— shall live under the sky without fear."[4]

Thus the Mohawks, the first of the tribes to accept the message of the Great Peace, became the founders of the Confederacy of Iroquois Tribal Nations.

It is significant that this pivotal point in the tale revolves around a tree. The tree is sacred in so many traditions, as the *axis mundi*, the spine of Gaia, the numinous agent of nature upon which one is stretched and tested. It is on the tree that the God-man of the West dies, gives up, leaps into absurdity in an ecstasy of agony. It is beneath a tree that the Man-god of the East sits, absurdly proclaiming, "I will not move from this tree until I have achieved enlightenment!" And while sitting there, in an agony of ecstasy, he indeed became enlightened. In the Native American tradition, it is in union with the tree that Deganawidah leaps into the void, certain of a new reality.

Interestingly, these three tree stories point up a significant difference between Western, Eastern, and Native American peoples. Jesus, dying on the tree, says, "My God, my God, why hast thou forsaken me?" It is a statement of relationship, of personality, and of intense interaction with God. The Buddha under the bodhi tree has so dissolved his "I" that even when demonic forces besiege him with seductions and lures, he says, "I cannot be seduced. I cannot be frightened. There's no longer any 'I.' And if there's no 'I,' there's no one to be seduced and nothing to be seduced by." Without identification in ego, the self dissolves into the All. With the Native peoples of the Americas as well as with many shamanic peoples, one bonds with the tree, because humankind is part of nature, and falls into the void, certain that nature will rescue and restore one.

In each case, of course, near death or actual extinction is followed by restoration and resurrection. In the Christian story, Jesus is resurrected as the Christ, the total personification of the God-man. Buddha arises from the tree as the selfless and compassionate Enlightened One who teaches others to go beyond grasping desire and suffering. In the Native American myth of Deganawidah, a man falls into the void on a tree, only to bring forth, in partnership with nature, a wholly new and natural way of being.

NOTES

[1] Ken Carey, *The Return of the Bird Tribes* (New York: Harper Collins, 1988), p. 92.

[2] Ibid., p. 93.

[3] Quoted in *The White Roots of Peace*, p. 22.

[4] Ibid., p. 22.

HACKING DOWN THE TREE OF FALSEHOOD

TIME: Sixty to ninety minutes.

MATERIALS: A drum (optional). A large room, with carpeting or mats, furnishings removed or moved to one side. Even better, a large private area outdoors. Writing materials or journals for each person to record thoughts and feelings after the "fall."

MUSIC: None. The Guide can, if she wishes, keep up a steady drumbeat during the hacking process.

INSTRUCTIONS FOR GOING SOLO: This process is easily done solo by following the instructions for chopping down the Tree of Falsehood. Try to imagine that you have witnesses to your action. Then, when it comes time to fall, make sure that you have a bed, a sofa, or some other soft place to land. Have a tape recorder or journal available to record your thoughts and feelings after you have "fallen."

SCRIPT FOR THE GUIDE:
In this powerful process we confront and physically hack away at those things in our life that we know to be false and which keep us from the higher truth of our lives. Then, when we feel we have cut through the branches and trunk of the tree of our own falsehood, we perform an act of trust and, like Deganawidah clasping the tree as it falls into the abyss, we fall backwards into the arms of our partners. This act signals our agreement to take the risk of leaving falseness behind and to begin to live by those nobler truths and finer actions in which we truly believe.

We have seen how Deganawidah chose to risk his life to persuade the Mohawks of the truth of his message of peace. By standing up in the Tree of War, the Tree of Falsehood, and by helping those who were hacking at the tree with their hatchets, he performed an act of sacred absurdity.

The absurd has a long and important history in the world's scriptures and myths—so much so, that it is often said that where the absurd is, there the gods are. One thinks of Abraham following the absurd command he had of Spirit to prove his devotion by sacrificing his only son Isaac, only to have an angel stay his hand. In many decks of Tarot cards, the Fool is shown stepping blithely out into an abyss. This image is often interpreted as a symbol of one's willingness to begin a spiritual journey. In Greek myth, Hercules agrees to the outlandish labors that Hera forces on him and, absurd as it seems, achieves all twelve of them. In this century, Mahatma Gandhi used only the forces of truth and passive resistance to win independence for India against contemptuous colonial justice and the crack regiments of the British Empire.

The absurd comes in strange and hallowed ways into our lives, bearing the numinous, carrying the force of new life and possibility. It calls us to go to our edges. It asks us to face the terrible fear of "looking like a fool" and urges us to go ahead and be one. Though people scoff or make fun of us, it is no matter. We become like St. Francis, fools for God. The absurd offers us the opportunity to risk and gamble everything for a larger return. Sometimes, our expected fall becomes a windfall. We cast our bread upon the waters, and it comes back sandwiches. We leap into the abyss, and the ground rises up to meet us.

We wager with the universe and, if we have sufficient faith and commitment, we win the bet. As a very young man, the great American psychologist William James, alone and sick in Europe without hope and direction, considered suicide. He was saved by reading of French philosopher Charles Renouvier's "wager" with the universe to live one month as if everything mattered and had meaning. James himself took the wager and, for one month, rose above his usual state of despondency and acted as if his life had meaning. At the end of the month, he had discovered new resources of strength and talent, changed his behavior and mood for the better, and returned to his studies in medicine and psychology. His subsequent psychology of "Pragmatism" and optimism has served to lift the despair of many people and bring them to a state of healthy-mindedness.

How many of you have done a foolhardy or ridiculous thing? What have you done that seemed at the time utterly absurd? Would each of you now please turn to a partner and share a story of an absurd thing that you did and its consequences. You each have about five minutes to tell your story of the absurd. (Ten minutes.)

As you may have discovered in telling your stories, our seemingly absurd actions often point to a higher truth about ourselves and our lives. But before this truth can manifest or be realized, we must often cut away the denial or self-deception that obscures it. In the Deganawidah story, the cutting away of falsehood is symbolized by hacking down a warped and distorted tree. I invite you now to ask yourself, what is false in me that needs cutting away? Is it a sense of inadequacy? Is it being conditioned and imprisoned by what other people think? Is it a sense of futility, an attitude that nothing will ever make a difference regardless of how hard I work?

(At this point, the Guide can invite participants to call out the falsehoods by which they have lived, such as "I'm too old," "I can't begin to live my life until my children are grown," or "I don't have the degrees to make a difference in the world." The Guide can also invite participants to speak of the fear of what might happen after they have cut down the tree of their own falsehoods and fallen into a new way of being. For example, "Once I make the leap, can I sustain the additional expectations?" or "I fear my old behavior will assert itself after the leap" or "I fear I'll be isolated, because I will have leaped beyond my friends." After this interval of discussion, the Guide continues as follows:)

Deganawidah's cutting down the tree of falsehood and falling into the gorge is in accord with a much-honored Native American tradition of risking or gambling everything for a higher goal. You know that you could lose everything you own—your money, your horses, your home—but still you feel safe because you know that your people are going to provide for you. You trust in Providence to catch you.

We are now about to emulate Deganawidah's action as literally as we can. To begin, would each of you now please find two other people who are close to your size and weight. (When everyone is in threes, the Guide will say:)

We are now going to experience each of the three roles of this process—the one who hacks away at the tree of their falsehood, the one who witnesses this action, and Providence which catches the falling one. If you are the person to fall, begin by chopping with an imaginary hatchet at the imaginary tree representing the false beliefs in your life. Put as much energy and vigor as you can into the act, speaking at the same time about what it is in your life that you are hacking away. Even if you are not entirely sure when you begin what the falsehood is, something about the process of hacking physically may bring it up into consciousness. Attack the falsehood you have chosen with all the fervor that you can muster until you are exhausted or until you are sure that it has been hacked away. Here is an example from Mystery School:

Participant (hacking vigorously): I am chopping away at the falsehood that tells me that nothing anybody does can matter to the world. I am hacking at the false belief that I am separate from everything. I'm chopping down the tree of falsehood that makes me afraid to dare. It keeps me a prisoner in its branches, telling me that the world is too dangerous and that nothing I can do will make any difference anyway. I know that this tree is killing me, and I'm going to chop it out of my life.

Another member of the threesome should act as the Witness. The Witness is totally present to the one who is chopping. Listen to what the person is willing to share about the falseness he or she is hacking away. Give encouragement to the chopper, urging the person to stay with it and continue chopping until he or she feels sure that the falsehood has been chopped away.

The third member of the group is the Catcher. You have the most important responsibility in the group because you represent the promise and the possibility that the act of falling will bring one to a higher knowledge or truth. You are the tangible fact that the fall is a risk work taking, that the universe will catch and support one who is willing to chop away falseness and fall into new being. If, for some reason, you let the person hit the ground, then you are reinforcing the fear that a truer life can't happen.

Prepare to make the catch by taking a broad stance about three feet behind the person who will fall (depending on his or her height). Your feet should be parallel to one another, not turned out, with the foot of your stronger leg slightly in front of the other one. Your knees should be slightly bent and your tail slightly dropped toward the floor. If, by any chance, the person who will be falling has a physical problem that might make a fall dangerous, the person must tell you, so that you can adjust the fall for them. A good way to do this is for both the Catcher and the Witness to gently turn and spiral the falling partner down to the ground.

When the person doing the chopping feels that he or she is ready to fall, the person should ask the Catcher, "Are you ready to catch me?" A "yes" answer that means that the catcher is ready to act as Providence. The person falling should extend his or her arms out to each side so that the Catcher has something to hook under.

The catch is done with the whole body. You hold your arms forward, ready to catch the falling person under the arms. As the person falls, step back slightly and bend, curving your back and bending your knees, so that you just take the person down gently. It is helpful to hook your elbows under the upper arms of the person falling.

Catching is serious business, for if you don't catch the one who falls, a whole lifetime of dreams may be compromised. But it's also important not to be too cautious. Don't grab the person after he or she has fallen only a few inches. Try to allow the person to fall at least a foot or more. The longer the person can fall safely, the more effective and powerful is the feeling of both risk and new possibility.

And those of you who are falling, go down backwards straight like a tree, without sticking your butt out to the floor. This may be tricky, but it's much safer and also kinder to the person you're falling toward. A straight fall also demonstrates that you're firm in your resolve, clear, and aware of exactly why you're falling. In Deganawidah's terms, you are falling into the other side of the rainbow, which can help you complete your life's purpose.

When you reach the ground and are lying there, you will speak of what you know after the fall. You may be aware of an entirely different state of consciousness. You may have new insights or even a different sense of purpose and possibility about your life—a life seen on the other side of the rainbow. Both the Witness and the Catcher will listen to what you have to say, and the Witness will record your remarks with paper and pen, occasionally prompting you to continue speaking about what you are discovering as a result of falling into new being. Here is an example from Mystery School:

Participant who has just fallen and is lying on the ground: I find that I have fallen into greenness, into a world that sustains and strengthens me. I'm not afraid anymore of the things in my past that have given me so much sorrow. I feel capable as I've never felt before.

Witness: What has happened to your Tree of Falsehood?

Participant (laughing): It's all toothpicks!

Begin now by choosing who will be the first one to hack at the tree, who will be the Witness, and who the Catcher. Please, hacker, give this activity plenty of vigor, speaking about what you are chopping away. Don't just go through the motions! This is a process that can have a critically important effect in your life, for what is done physically and symbolically can reach into and uproot old habits and patterns in ways that are truly remarkable.

After the first partner has fallen and spoken of the world beyond the fall, each of you will stand up, stretch, and then the next partner will begin hacking, with other members of the trio cycling through the roles. You may wish to take a short break after each of your partners has completed the hacking and falling. I will be available to assist any group that feels it needs another Catcher to be on the safe side. You have thirty to forty minutes to go through the entire process, with each of you having a turn in all three of the roles. When all have gone through the process, please sit quietly and write in your notebooks or reflect on what you have discovered about falling, witnessing, and catching. Begin now. (Thirty to forty minutes.)

(At the end of this process, there should be a celebration of what has been accomplished, with music, dance, jokes, and splendid food.)

GRIEF AND ITS LIFTING

T he story now moves back to the adventures of Hiawatha, the great orator on fire with the New Mind. Deganawidah had asked Hiawatha to work among his own people, the Onondaga nation, and especially to try to convert the wizard chieftain, Tadodaho.

Tadodaho was brilliant, with an evil intelligence that could always discern people's weaknesses and play upon them. In some versions of the story, including the one told here, he had already done terrible damage to Hiawatha's life. He seemed to summon up the worst in people and then use this power for his own ends and to his victims' shame. Many young warriors were in his thrall, acting, it seemed, without conscience. His appearance was calculated to strike terror: matted and spiky hair, which is why people said he had snakes in his hair, and a twisted and contorted body. In the light of today's psychoanalytic knowings, we think of what must have happened to him as a child to deform his body, and why having a twisted body led to his having a monstrous, twisted mind—or the reverse. Tadodaho was said to be so powerful that he could kill opponents from a distance through sorcery and invade people's dreams at night with terrifying images of torture and murder. Cannibalism was but one atrocity in his catalogue of horrors. People who opposed him died in enigmatic ways. An archetype of evil power, like Hitler, Stalin, or certain Mafia chiefs, he assumed a command over people's psyches great enough to destroy any notions of peace. His terrorist warriors made life miserable not only for the Onondaga people but also for the nearby Cayuga and Seneca villagers farther west.

Hiawatha began his mission by sending messages to all of the Onondaga settlements, inviting them to attend a council at which he, with his great oratorical skills, would present his proposals for a New Mind and a Great Peace. On the day appointed for the council, the people waited around the council fire in great numbers, hoping for the message that would end their sorrow and pain. Just as the meeting was about to begin, Tadodaho appeared. He said nothing, but his presence was so ferocious and his negative charisma so potent that he intimidated everyone. Tadodaho just stood there and looked at the people who had come to hear Hiawatha's message. Silently, his dark warriors and assistant wizards moved through the crowd, looking from face to face. Fearfully, the people dispersed before Hiawatha could say a word.

Shortly thereafter, the eldest of Hiawatha's three remaining daughters became sick with an illness that refused to respond to treatment. Soon she died, and many suspected that her death was the result of Tadodaho's sorcery. Grief stricken but still refusing to surrender the Great Plan for Peace, Hiawatha called a second council. It is interesting to notice that grief in this story is over the death of daughters, not sons. In most other legends, it is generally a dying son who inspires grief. But in the Iroquois culture in which women were so honored, the death of daughter was as much a matter for grieving as the loss of a son, if not more so, because women were capable of bringing new life into the world.

Fewer people appeared at Hiawatha's second council. Again those who did were filled with terror at the presence of Tadodaho and his warriors, and again they left without hearing the Good News. Following the second council, Hiawatha's second daughter fell into a mysterious illness and died. Again, people attributed the death to the evil sorcery of Tadodaho. In many stories of mythic power in which light and dark confront each other, the dark always wins in the early stages. Even Hiawatha, though not damaged in his body, felt his mind becoming more and more afflicted by these horrible events. We remember that he had been originally wounded in his mind and spirit when he had tried to persuade Tadodaho to change his ways. As a result of Tadodaho's sorcery and the loss of four of his daughters, he had taken up cannibalism himself, like his enemy. Now the same wounding was returning and, in the same manner as before, the old hurts, the old pathology was rising in him again.

Some of Hiawatha's followers among the Onondaga approached Tadodaho in canoes, hoping to talk to him. In some tellings, they were drowned by the waves—symbolically, the waves of negativity sent out by Tadodaho. In others, they found themselves fighting amongst themselves, the prospect of facing such a horrendous force of evil creating dissension and chaos among them.

Day and night Hiawatha could hear Tadodaho's voice crying out his name in an eerie shamanic chant, "HI-A-WA-THA-A-A-A-A!" The sound pierced his soul. Nevertheless, he refused to abandon his efforts and, after the end of his mourning period for his second daughter, Hiawatha called a third council. This time he took his third and youngest daughter, who was his dearest friend and the closest companion of his heart. Hiawatha hoped that if he kept her near him, she would not get sick.

As the delegates gathered, the women went off to collect firewood for the cooking. Hiawatha's daughter, who was pregnant, begged her father to let her accompany them. As she walked to the edge of the clearing, a great bird—some say an eagle—appeared in the sky. Seeing it, Tadodaho pointed upward, and immediately one of his archers shot the bird. The eagle fell to earth near where Hiawatha's daughter was collecting firewood. There was a wild melee, as people, consumed by greed, raced to the spot to tear out the eagle's much valued feathers. In their mindless rush, they trampled and killed the young woman and her unborn child.

This time Hiawatha's grief knew no bounds, and no one was capable of comforting him. Perhaps the Onondaga had become so accustomed to the tragedy of death that they had lost touch with one another's grief. We recognize this numbness in our own times as we watch and read the media's daily horror show, with news of local rape and rapine preceding news of mass killings, drug wars, and the genocide of nations. Switch the channel and, more often than not, you will find a dramatization of the above, blurring the distinction between cruel fiction and even crueler fact. With these visions constantly before us, the evil that people do seems to be part of some surreal theatrical, a grotesque but scripted Grand Guignol of planetary proportions. Our capacity for empathy thus deadened, is it any wonder that we feel our humanity dwindle?

This latest tragedy shattered Hiawatha. As the traditional storytellers describe it, he wept over his favorite daughter, saying, "I have now lost all my daughters. In the death of this, my last daughter, Tadodaho, you have killed two beings, my daughter and the child that was within her."[1] Overcome with grief and despair, Hiawatha left the land of the Onondaga and began a long and lonely journey away into the forest, his mind becoming more and more distorted. He felt that he was losing the essential noble character which he had regained during his time with Deganawidah. Once again the evil soul of Tadodaho seemed to be filling him like an incubus, twisting his spirit, scarring his mind, turning him away from his new work of bringing in the Great Law, and making any form of peace seem impossible.

Only nature offered Hiawatha any consolation, and it was to nature that he turned for wisdom and comfort. Because his Deep Face had been seen by Deganawidah, he was not the same Hiawatha who had been so hideously wounded the first time. So in this time of profound grief, even though his pathology tried to assert itself, he did not fall into the pattern of his previous criminal behavior. Instead he fell into nature. As he wandered, Hiawatha came to the beautiful area of the Tully Lakes, where the ducks were thick on the water. Here he was able to witness—some say to cause—a magical event. Like many of us during soul-charged times, he was drawn to the water. "By the waters of Babylon they sat down and wept," goes the old song. But when Hiawatha carried his grief to the lakeside, something utterly wondrous happened. As the ducks spread their wings and lifted off, they carried all the lake's water with them on their webbed feet. We can imagine Hiawatha's feelings as he crossed the lake with dry moccasins. The lifting up into the heavens of water perhaps put into his mind the possibility of lifting the waters of grief and offering them to the Spirit of the sky. As he crossed the now-dry lake, he saw all that had been previously hidden. Drawn by their brightness, he bent down to pick up some shells from the lake bottom. These, some say, were the shells he made into beads to use in the creation of wampum, those strings of beads that the Iroquois use to commemorate their stories and to speak truth.

As the traditional story tells it, Hiawatha continued on his travels carrying his shells and came one morning upon a stand of elderberry rushes. He cut the rushes into three lengths and strung them with shell beads. Then he cut two forked sticks and planted them in the ground, placing a small pole across them. He lay the three strings over the pole, while saying to himself, "This would I do if I found anyone burdened with grief even as I am. I would console them, for they would be covered with night and wrapped in darkness. This would I lift with words of condolence; these strings of beads would become words with which I would address them." This, the Iroquois say, is the origin of their ritual of condolence, practiced as a way to mourn with and to comfort those in grief, even to the present day.

Then Hiawatha wandered, bereft, scarcely knowing where he traveled. Occasionally he camped outside a settlement, but no one came to comfort him—to lift the strings of condolence. So it is with ourselves. The grief-stricken seem to have an invisible barrier around them which we lack the courage to penetrate. We do what we can but aren't eager "to intrude," as we call it, on their grief.

When Hiawatha reached the edge of the forest near one of the Mohawk villages, he sat down upon the stump of a fallen tree—some say the same tree from which Deganawidah had fallen. A woman passed by him and, seeing him sitting there, returned to her village and said, "A man—or a figure like a man—is seated by the spring with his breast covered with strings of white shells."

That night, Deganawidah, who was now living in the Mohawk village, went to the place where the smoke from Hiawatha's fire was seen rising. As he approached, he saw Hiawatha meditating on the condolence strings which were hanging on the pole before him and heard Hiawatha saying again the words, "This would I do if I found anyone burdened with grief, even as I am. I would take these shell strings in my hand and condole with him. The strings would become words and lift away the darkness with which the person is covered. Holding these in my hand, my words would be true."

Then Deganawidah came forward and, lifting the strings from the horizontal pole, he held each strand, one after the other and spoke the words of what are called the Requickening Address. These words have been used ever since by people of the Iroquois nation in their ceremony of condolence. They comprise one of the most powerful psychological and spiritual remedies for grief that I have ever heard.

Presenting the first string, Deganawidah said, "When a person has suffered a great loss caused by death and is grieving, tears blind his eyes so that he cannot see. With these words I wipe away the tears from your face, using the white fawn skin of compassion, so that now you may see clearly. I make it daylight for you. I beautify the sky. Now shall you do your thinking in peace when your eyes rest on the sky, which the Perfector of our Faculties, the Master of All Things, intended should be a source of happiness to humans."

Presenting the second string, Deganawidah said, "When a person has suffered a great loss caused by death and is grieving, there is an obstruction in his ears, and he cannot hear. With these words I remove the obstruction from your ears so that you may once again have perfect hearing."

Presenting the third string, he said, "When a person has suffered a great loss caused by death and is grieving, his throat is stopped, and he cannot speak. With these words I remove the obstruction from your throat so that you may speak and breathe freely."[2]

With these three basic statements of the condolence ceremony, Hiawatha's mind was freed from its sorrow, or rather, from its incessant dwelling on sorrow and grief. When the ceremony was completed, Hiawatha's mind was healed, and he and Deganawidah looked upon each other with wonder and astonishment. Hiawatha saw Deganawidah as the incarnation of goodness and fineness of spirit, and Deganawidah saw Hiawatha as the possible human, a strong and righteous man with many talents and extraordinary courage. Together they could advance the New Mind and spread the Good News to all the nations.

Deganawidah then invited Hiawatha to help him create the new laws of the Great Peace. For each foundation idea, they created a string or a belt of wampum, using the condolence beads in a new way to enable them to remember ideas without writing. After this time, the Iroquois used different bead designs to help them remember a speech, a treaty, a set of commitments or ideas, a constitution. In fact, the constitution of the Iroquois Confederacy was essentially written in wampum beads. This is why the gift of a wampum string held immense value for Native peoples. In the great councils people who wanted to speak would stand up holding the wampum that held the memory of the points they wished to make. They would work through the beads making their points and then lay the string in the center on the pole. The next speaker would pick up the beads of the previous speaker to refer to and review the points that had been made and then add points of his or her own. As the council created a new treaty or agreement, its members would work together on the wampum, weaving in each new statement, each new knowing of their collective intention. It was a tremendous idea. When a speaker held the wampum, he or she could not lie because of the force of tradition held in the wampum beads of truth. The treaties of the white men were just scribbles on a page that could be destroyed; whereas the wampum beads were real, an art which stood for consciousness, reality, and commitment.

Wearing the wampum belts in which were coded the foundation of the New Peace, Daganawidah and Hiawatha traveled forth as partners, visiting over the next five years the tribes of the west, the Oneidas, the Onondagas, the Cayugas, and the Senecas. As they journeyed, accompanied by the chiefs of the Mohawk nation, they sang the peace hymn, a hymn of thanksgiving, also known as the "Six Songs." It is sung even today. Here is the Mohawk version. Other versions, including the Onondaga, extend the thanks to the

children, the plants and animals, the growing seasons, and to all
living things.

The Peace Hymn

or

Hail! Hail!

(The Six Songs)

Hai! Hai! Hai!
Hail! Hail! Hail!
  Once more we come to greet and thank the League;
  Once more to greet and thank the nations' Peace.
    Hai, hai, hai, hai, hai!
    Hail, hail, hail, hail, hail!

Hail! Hail! Hail!
  Once more we come to greet and thank the Kindred;
  Once more to greet and thank the dead chief's Kindred.
    Hail, hail, hail, hail, hail!

Hail! Hail! Hail!
  Once more we come to greet the Warriors;
  Once more to greet and thank the nation's Manhood.
    Hail, hail, hail, hail, hail!

Hail! Hail! Hail!
  Once more we come to greet and thank the Women;
  Once more to greet and thank the mourning Women.
    Hail, hail, hail, hail, hail!

Hail! Hail! Hail! that which our Forefathers accomplished!
Hail! Hail! Hail! the Law our Forefathers established!

O listen to us, listen, continue to hear us, our Grandsires!
O listen to us, listen, continue to hear us, our Grandsires![3]

NOTES

[1] This quote is in Barbara Graymount's excellent account of the Deganawidah story and is found in her book *Iroquois* (New York: Chelsea House, 1988) p. 19. Graymount's study is recommended as one of the best general introductions not only to this story but also to Iroquois history and culture.

[2] The full story, its ceremonial power and the words spoken are described in many sources, but very beautifully in Wallace, *The White Roots of Peace*, pp. 23–25.

[3] Ibid., p. 41.

TELLING THE CONDOLENCE BEADS

TIME: Sixty to ninety minutes.

MATERIALS: A wide assortment of beads, some large, some small (at least seven per participant) and leather or plastic string of the right thickness to fit through the beads.

MUSIC: Native American flute music.

INSTRUCTIONS FOR GOING SOLO: As this process involves the lifting of grief by another, it is best done with one other person. If that is not possible, then follow the instructions and play both parts in front of a mirror.

SCRIPT FOR THE GUIDE:

PART ONE

In this process, we will work with both the condolence ceremony and the wampum belt of memory. We will be following the parts in the story in which Hiawatha wove the three strands of beads for his dead daughters and Deganawidah lifted his grief by speaking words of condolence to him. Each bead that we place on our string will have its own story, and we will work with them until their full story is revealed. When your strand is complete, you can use it like wampum to remember each incident, each belief, each part of the deep message of the past. Your condolence string can be something that you can hold forever. You can make it a bracelet, or you can just keep it with you. When you are holding it, you cannot lie or, to put it a better way, you will tell true.

The Iroquois people say about the wampum, "This belt preserves my words." So when you take your string of beads home, it becomes the witness to your words. Every time you see the string, your words are preserved in it. The Iroquois also say, "The wampum is our heart." So the heart and the word become one in the beads.

Two beautiful qualities of the Native American tradition are illustrated in this process. The first is that while Native Americans seem to speak metaphorically, they actually bring their metaphors and symbols into reality. Thus, when Deganawidah says, "I hack down a Tree of Falsehood," he's using an image, but he also physically hacks down a tree. Later when Deganawidah announces that he will plant a Tree of Peace, his beautiful metaphor also becomes a physical action. So when we say that our griefs and losses are beads on the string of our life, we are speaking in images, but we also will use our hands to string real beads which hold our memories. The second beautiful quality is that in the Native American tradition you don't have to be stuck with a single version of the truth. Just as there are many tellings of the Deganawidah legend, all of them in some sense true, so too the beads that you string can change their meanings over time, and each meaning will be a true one. As you hold the beads and feel the power stored in them, they change and grow, and that's as it should be. In making your condolence string, you will be making a living thing which brings you into closer connection with the Mind of the Maker.

So would you just begin to think now about what you want to bead into your wampum. Those of us who have suffered losses will want to have a bead for each loss. So begin, please, by coming over to the table where the beads and string are, pick up one piece of string, and choose the beads you would like to string—or, rather, let the beads choose you.

As you place the beads on the string, hold in your mind the meaning each bead has for you. So, for example, I am stringing these three beads. (The Guide can substitute explanations of her own for the beads she is stringing, or she can read the following example:

In the green one I am seeing my laughing father who died a few years ago and for whose death I still feel very strongly. And on the red I am seeing my great mastiff dog who died recently who had been the great friend of my life. And in the black bead I'm seeing a friend who I did not know very well, but who became very dear at the end of her life.)

The sorrows you bead into your wampum do not necessarily have to be for those who have died. A bead can stand for something that has been lost or released in your life that has been part of your life for a long time. Or it can just be a dark or negative quality of mind that you want to lift in yourself. But each bead should be a very profound statement of meditation. (Again, the Guide can substitute explanations of her own for the beads she is stringing, or she can read the following example:

This white bead stands for the relationship with my mother that never worked out. This carved brown bead stands for the hopes I once had for a career in advertising that I abandoned when I married and had children. And this purple bead stands for the persistence of melancholy in my life.)

So begin, please, by picking up one piece of string and choosing your beads. Then, knot one end of the strand and begin to string your beads.

(When all the members of the group have finishing stringing their beads, the Guide will say:) Now that we have strung our beads, we will use them as Deganawidah did to lift Hiawatha's excessive grief and to give condolence. Would everyone please choose a partner and sit down together. To begin, one person holds his or her beads and tells the partner what they stand for.

I will now read you an example of a condolence ceremony that was done at Mystery School using the beads, and then you will do your own.

Woman participant: The first one, this red bead, stands for my sense of deep loss about my husband, the twentieth anniversary of whose death I marked just last week. So he's really strong in my memory. He was a supportive, powerful, understanding male figure in my life, and I still feel his loss. And then I have these little white beads which are my in-between years which I spent doing nothing, working and trying to forget. And this brown bead is the farm that I grew up on, and the soil, the south Texas soil, that is part of my makeup and which I have left behind. And this green bead is the acceptance speech I'll never give for the Oscar I'll never win.

When you have finished speaking, your partner will take your beads, hold them up, and with great respect, use them to touch first your eyes, then your ears, then your throat. As she does, she will say words such as these: "I, as the witness of your griefs, hold your beads of memory, and I say: With these beads I lift the darkness from your eyes, so that you can see your life and your losses with new vision. With these beads, I unblock your ears so that you can hear deeply and with new clarity your own words and those of others. And with these beads I clear the obstruction from your throat and from your breath so that you are capable of full expression and full inspiration and can speak powerfully of your sufferings and your joys. Now, please tell me again what these beads mean."

You can vary the words to suit your own form of expression. Just try to keep the same intention. (The Guide should read the words of condolence several times more so that the participants will learn the form of the condolence ceremony.)

Let one person tell her beads and receive condolence from the other. Then the second person will tell his or her beads and receive condolence. You each have five minutes to tell your beads and to receive the ceremony of condolence. (Ten minutes.)

After both partners have been consoled, you will each tell your beads again, this time allowing them to reveal their full story. Here is an example:

Woman participant: This red bead is the passionate laughter of life that my late husband had, and that I still hear. And it also stands

for not just the love that I felt for him, but the love he felt for me.
So I feel that love burn red again. And the little white years since
his death are turned now to peace. And the soil of south Texas is
the root of my being that I no longer deny. And the Oscar speech
I'll never give is transformed to thanks to everybody for everything.

Each person now should ask his or her partner to tell the full story
the beads, the story that is revealed after the condolence ceremony
and the lifting of the grief. Would you please now take turns and
tell your beads again to each other, this time speaking of the larger
story that is revealed after the grief has been lifted. New insights
may appear as well as a reconciliation and peace with what before
had given you only regret and sorrow. You each have five minutes
to tell each other the larger story as you discover it in each bead.
(Ten minutes.)

You have combined the condolence ceremony with the honoring
and lifting of your whole life—not just lifting your sorrows, your
pains, but also, if you will, remythologizing your life, deepening its
story. This is perhaps as powerful a training as any on how to release
pain. In the future, if you want to console someone who's really
suffering, you may find it beneficial not just to stay with the suffering
but to look also at the qualities of life implicit in the suffering and
release these qualities to bring in a larger story.

PART TWO

Now, in this second part of the process, we are going to use our
beads like wampum to tell our stories in their fullness to each other.
In the Native American tradition, when you tell the wampum beads,
you tell the truth of your knowings over and over again. Often when
you decide to meet another person at a more profound level, you
begin the relationship by handing him or her your wampum and
telling your life from the beads. Then the person understands and
appreciates you at a depth that transcends mere acquaintance.

So we are going to wander about the room now, and we're going
to stop before someone with whom we perhaps have never talked

deeply before and ask this person to tell us his or her beads. For example, I might say, "Would you tell me your beads?" And she might reply, "This is the laughter of joy. This is years of peace. This is the ground of my being which is the earth. This is the capacity to feel gratitude for everything." And then I might say, "I affirm that you have told me true." Then she will say to me, "Now, would you tell me your beads?" And I might reply, "This is the flame of energy and of the call that flares through my life. This blue bead is the sorrow that continuously deepens it. The green is the greening of my mind. The brown bead is the things that ground me—nature, brown dogs, brown books, chocolate, the antiquities that are very important to me." And she will affirm that I have told true.

And then, thanking each other, you will move around the room until you find another person to whom to tell your beads. As you continue to do this, allow your beads to give you new insights. Thus what you tell the next person may be somewhat different from what you told the previous one. Your story, like all stories, keeps growing and deepening.

So in a moment, you will begin to wander, finding people with whom to share the telling of the beads. Remember to affirm the truth of the telling to each other. If you meet someone who is grieving, you can offer condolence, using his or her beads to lift the sorrow. And if you are in need of condolence, you can ask for it from the people you meet. You may find that the story the beads tell will change from person to person, but each telling will be a true one. Begin. (Ten to fifteen minutes.)

(At the completion of this process, the Guide will invite everyone, to say a word of gratitude for all the experiences that make up a life. Then the Guide will say:)

And so you see, our life story, like all great stories, keeps deepening and enriching as it is told. As you tell your stories in their fullness, you see that you have a pattern and a path of life, and you begin to access the understanding that energizes and clarifies the potentials of that path. People who do not reflect on their lives and tell their stories in different ways often lose their sense of the deeper qualities and meanings that underlie the pattern and drama of their lives. But now you have a new method for understanding your lives and the lives of others, one that you can take out into the world of your family or friends, even into your professional life. This can result in many benefits. Not only will you be understood and appreciated at a deeper level but you will come to understand and appreciate others more richly and stop taking them for granted. Most important, as you tell your beads or your stories over and over again in many variations and in many different ways, you affirm and enrich the pattern of your life and find yourself more deeply attentive to its unfolding.

7

A LARGER CIRCLE OF ALLIES

▲▲

Most accounts of the story that have been set down outside the oral tradition cover the next period in a few sentences. They describe how Deganawidah and Hiawatha brought unity and peace to the powerful Mohawk tribe and then began their peace mission to neighboring tribes. We hear that the two men were adopted into the Mohawk nation, the People of the Flint. Flint, used to make arrows and other tools, gave Mohawk warriors an edge over nearby tribes, so it was strategically appropriate that they became the first people to take hold of the Great Peace. News that the Mohawk leaders and people had embraced the New Mind must have been a powerful and persuasive lure for other tribes.

The story implies that a ground swell for peace began moving through the land. News spread of the miracle of Deganawidah's stone canoe and his survival of the fall as well as the conversion of the Mohawks, who had been the most feared of warriors. Other tribes also wondered about the new condolence ceremonies that lifted grief from people's hearts. And since nothing travels faster than a song, the Peace Hymn swept through the tribes, igniting council fires of hope and filling the hearts and minds of people with a joyous expectancy for a new era among the five nations.

The Peacemakers were coming! The Peacemakers were coming! And indeed they came, singing the great Peace Hymn as they traveled forth to the tribes of the west, the Oneidas, the Onondagas, the Cayugas, the Senecas. As they went along, more and more allies joined them, including the chiefs of the other Mohawk tribes. Lest peace sound like a foregone conclusion, we must keep in mind the gifts the two men brought and consider some of the demands of such work, for it is at this point on the journey at which we, too, as Peacemakers will require the utmost courage and steadfastness.

The first gift, of course, was the power of vision. Deganawidah encouraged people to cocreate the vision, to think deeply about the details of the peaceful and potent society they were dreaming collectively into being. At each new location, the Peacemakers asked the people to share their own ideas and thoughts about how to advance the triple message of Righteousness, Health, and Power. Only the worthiest of visions could be sustained during such a long period of day-to-day work. Thus the great questions of polity were asked and explored together: How best to live with cooperation, mutual respect, and interdependence to assure the blessings of a just and righteous society? How best to create health of mind and body in order to remember that the worst enemy lies within and not in the other and that to be whole one must practice, nourish, and exemplify wholeness? How best to celebrate the spiritual power that moves within and between all beings, to tap into its infinite resources, discover its rituals and ceremonials, and become an instrument and working partner of the Great Spirit? Above all, how to continue to practice, maintain, and manifest peace in all one's relations?

The second gift of the Peacemakers was timing. Success demands that we recognize and seize the open moment when things are ripe for change and the world is ready for renovation. Deganawidah arrived at the moment of most profound need, but he also knew how to wait, when to move, and what to do at each moment. For many of us, this is another point when we risk losing heart or allowing our energies for the radical task to leak away. When we misstep, or rush in too quickly without adequate preparation—that is, without having already practiced in our own lives the arts and skills of peace and thus lack the power of conviction and the passion of persuasion that such practice brings—we risk failure. Our nerve can also fail, or we can falter from the sheer exhaustion that comes of trying to shore up old institutions with new ideas, of trying to put new wine into old bottleskins. The gift of timing also brings with it the knowledge of where and with whom the open moment can be found. Then one can go to work with those who are ready to engage the difficult task of dissolving the old and preparing the new. These people of the right moment often bring valuable new insights, talents ready to bloom, and a freshness of perspective to the process of change. This is surely one of the reasons Deganawidah and Hiawatha shared the message with all who were ready and willing to hear it, so that not only would the message gain in strength, but the allies could bring skills and awareness to the task that the two principle Peacemakers might lack. Truly great social artists always know that they carry only a piece of the vision, and the empowerment of others to bring in the rest is what peacemaking and worldmaking are all about.

Then, too, Deganawidah and Hiawatha honed their skills at timing with the same energy and sense of life-and-death importance that a party of legendary warriors might bring to a major battle plan. This is another piece of information useful to us. A Peacemaker can transmute into new life and hope energies and skills that may have been used to plot death and mayhem. Whereas Hitler employed brilliant but devious creative energy to wreak havoc and call down holocaust, Gandhi used the great creative energies of love to make peace and evoke a spiritual power that continues to have the widest consequences in all corners of the globe. In this spirit, Deganawidah's peace troupe came singing, telling stories, offering symbols and cer-emonies to quicken the mind and heart of the hearers. The news of this glorious band went before them, and when they came into settlements and villages, the gifts that they offered of creativity and cocreation surpassed all expectation.

Today we are accustomed to hyperbole, to the world according to advertising, fast-cut media images of all desires fulfilled, all fantasies realized. As a result, we have grown cynical from continuous disap-pointment at the failure of the product to live up to the surreal prom-ise. What, then, can we learn from the persistent, person-to-person, village-to-village, tribe-to-tribe work of Deganawidah, Hiawatha, and their allies? Perhaps it is that there is no substitute for a practical, everyday encounter with the vision, trusting that a truth will grow stronger as it is passed along, never weaker. When massive disappointment comes, as it ultimately did for the Iroquois, what then? Deganawidah, as we shall see, allowed in his great vision even for that.

But the most potent offerings of the men and women bringing peace were the ever-present sense of gratitude for life in all its aspects and the ceremonies of condolence and quickening, which for the first time offered a way out of the cycle of vengeance. Before Deganawidah's dream took hold, bloody raids and retribution were an expected part of tribal life. What a change it brought to have one's beloved family members mourned in ceremony and to be gently reminded that obsessive grieving damaged the creative power of life, especially when it locked one into thoughts of revenge. Instead, one was invited to remember that the beauty of the world still existed, that the truth of one's love could be woven into strands of beads and kept safe forever, and that the sorrow of one's heart could be spoken and lifted, with balance and beauty restored to one's life. The ceremony of the lifting of grief which the Peacemakers created changed the Iroquois world and could, perhaps, change ours.

Recently, I visited Pearl Harbor and joined a large group of tourists, Americans and Japanese, who were ferried across the harbor to stand on the memorial built over the spot where the *Arizona* sank. We were shown a powerful film of the Japanese attack on December 7, 1941. We knew that thousands of American soldiers and sailors had lost their lives in the attack, the largest number on the *Arizona*. Most of these men's bodies were trapped under the water, entombed in the remains of the great ship. A tubelike structure rose from the sunken ship, joining the world of the dead to that of the living. The names of those who had died were inscribed on a beautiful tablet. At first there was tension in the air between the Americans and Japanese. How does one act under such circumstances? What does one say? Then, spontaneously, many Japanese lifted the flowery leis that were hanging around their necks, went to the tablet and, with prayers, laid their wreaths under the names of the dead. Others placed their leis within the tube and bowed to the American dead. A deep sympathy moved among all present. Here was a healing, a ceremony for a new world, an enormous act of love and condolence. What Deganawidah and Hiawatha had begun so many centuries before was continuing among peoples who had suffered the greatest woundings from each other.

Bearing these gifts, Deganawidah, Hiawatha, and their growing band of allies traveled first to the Oneidas, the People of the Standing Stones. What were these stones that one finds dotted throughout the northeast? Some archaeologists say they are counterparts on these shores of the standing stones that are to be found running from the British Isles down to Spain. Was this tradition brought, perhaps, by ancient European sailors, or are the stones a testament to a need of peoples wherever they are to erect stones that are charged with special significance? Whether astronomical markings or sacred sites, the standing stones remain a mystery. We are certain, however, that one particular dolmanlike stone held the spiritual center for the Oneidas. From the place of their sacred standing stone, the Oneidas readily accepted the Great Peace, sponsored as it was by their neighbors, the Mohawks.

Then Deganawidah and his allies came again to the land of the Onondagas, the People on the Hill. As they approached, they were met by the paralyzing cry of the wizard Tadodaho, "*HWE-DO-NE-E-E-EH?*" ("When will this be?") The negative energy of Tadodaho's resistance forced the peace emissaries to leave the Onondaga yet again and to approach instead the Cayugas, known as the Great Height People because their lands encompassed cliffs as well as fertile lowlands near the river waters. The Cayugas, known for their helpfulness and gentle ways, were overjoyed to take hold of the Great Peace and embrace its concepts and laws.

So now, with three nations supporting them, Deganawidah and his allies returned again to the Onondagas. Over a period of years, they were able to persuade the Onondaga chiefs—all but Tadodaho— that it would be in their best interest to join the rapidly forming league. Accompanied by the chiefs of four nations, the Mohawks,

the Oneidas, the Onondagas, and the Cayugas, they walked, singing
the Peace Hymn, to Canandaigua Lake. There, with their enormous
gifts of oratory and persuasion, the gathered allies convinced two
warring branches of the People of the Great Hill, the battle-loving
Senecas, whose greatest joy for generations had been to fight among
themselves, to end their feuding and to join the League.

Now all the chiefs of the five nations were assembled. It is important to note That the word *chief* is an inadequate translation of
the title *sachem*, which really means "the one who does good" or
"the one whose care is for all." Together with these "ones who
do good," Deganawidah and Hiawatha were ready to return to
Onondaga Lake where the one dissenting chief, the one who did
evil, dwelled. Deganawidah said, "We must seek the fire and look
for the smoke of Tadodaho. He alone stands across our path. His
mind is twisted, and there are seven crooks in his body. These must
be straightened if the League is to endure."

We are today in a time which requires the building of new leagues
and partnerships across governments, companies, arts, sciences, religions, and ways of being. The need to foster international and
cross-cultural partnership is the same today as it was in the Peacemaker's time, but on an enormously expanded scale. How do we
in the Planetary Longhouse learn to honor the different perspectives
on Righteousness, Health, and Spiritual Power that come from the
experience and lore of other cultures? How do we learn to listen
to ways of knowing that evolved in a different manner and with
different emphasis? We need to cultivate the habit of multicultural
deep listening that provides for an ecology of cultures, and we need
to ask the right questions: How do Africans think, walk, dream?
How do Chinese understand the nature of the Tao, the flow of
things? How do the Eskimos see complete models of inner imagery,
and the Balinese develop such remarkable capacity to perform and
perfect many artistic forms? Our growing multicultural awareness
is giving us perspectives and learnings that are no longer limited to
a particular place and culture; they are becoming available to the
whole family of humankind. In this great "howness," we stand to

be enriched on a scale that is virtually mythic. We are privileged to live in the time of the great harvest of the learnings of many different peoples over vast expanses of space and time. This time brings confusion and ambiguity, but it also brings seedings from other climes and minds, plantings that make for unique growth and singular fruit. Because of the meshing and meeting of cultures, we are entering the biggest "jump phase" in human history, so much so that if we continue on this path toward peace and avoid self-destruction, it may be that several hundred years from now, our descendents will look back on us as honored, if primitive, founders of the earthwide Longhouse and, like the Iroquois, sing hymns of praise and peace in remembrance of what we tried to do.

On a personal level, we are already in some sense participating in a multicultural global society, although some of us may experience it as conflict. I am referring to the fact that many people in North America are the product of many bioregions and races, each with a particular genius and potential. Sometimes these differences require mediation and inner peacemaking before we are able to harvest and weave these varying cultural legacies into a new form.

My own heritage is a cross between Scotch and Sicilian (a place that has been invaded and colonized for thousands of years, resulting in a confluence in the blood of most of the European, Mediter-ranean, and North African peoples.) Additionally, on my father's side, I am one-eighth Cherokee. I often feel both a complementarity and a dissension between the radically differing cultures and ways of understanding moving around inside me. Many people alive on the planet today are embodiments of this kind of "hybrid vigor." But it is possible to work within for a Great Peace, not unlike Deganawidah's, so that our many internal forms of culture live in amity, promoting productive exchange and deep ecology. The essential requirement then as well as now, within as well as without, is that all groups or cultures recognize the genius and sovereignty of each, and that the stronger or economically dominant culture not attempt to subjugate or disenfranchise the others. Our task in this dynamic dance of cultures is to be fascinated and inspired by our differences, to learn and grow from them. Occasionally we will be overwhelmed, but mostly we will be enchanted.

So it is for the many nations we meet in our neighbors and colleagues. Such multicultural blending or weaving is, perhaps, the genius of the Americas, which provides in the society for a confluence of potentials and quickenings which parallels the confluence in the body/mind of its people. Moreover, the American vision of accessing the best of many cultures is now the task of the world as a whole. Many visionaries are trying to create on the world stage a confederacy which honors the different potentials of all nations and also elicits from them a deeper sharing in order to form a multicultural world society guided by substantially new premises. In such a world, we harvest the old traditions, but are not dependent upon them; we honor the constitutions, parliaments, and declarations of independence, but also use them as springboards to the affirmation of interdependence and to forms of governance in which all think globally as they act locally. As Deganawidah and his allies were, so are we now are at that stumbling, startling, shining open moment— ready to declare the depth, the breadth, the scope of the vision of the Great Peace.

Once we have surrounded ourselves with a circle of allies and harvested the many perspectives they offer to the task, we can take on our major challenge. In the Deganawidah story, this challenge is represented by Tadodaho, without whose compliance a true peace could not come into being. He stood for everything that obstructed the way of peace: tremendous negative charisma; static and unmoving power; autocracy, including the inner autocracy of the ego; unwillingness to change; hunger for power and control; and the deep wounding that leads a person to wound the rest of the world. Tadodaho was so twisted he wanted the rest of the world to be twisted. Since time out of mind, humans have believed that it is possible to destroy an enemy to win our goals. Tadodaho, however, was indestructible; he could be neither killed nor nullified. This story teaches us, then, that so-called enemies need not be destroyed; they can be transformed.

How Deganawidah and Hiawatha dealt with him is a telling and trenchant allegory of what we can do when we are similarly oppressed by apparently implacable forces, whether they come from outside ourselves, or from our own inner Tadodaho. First, according to some versions, the Peacemakers consulted Jigonhsasee, who helped them form a plan to heal, persuade, and even transform and empower Tadodaho so that he would serve the Great Peace. Guided by the Mother of Nations, Deganawidah and Hiawatha prepared to use a combination of therapeutic methods on Tadodaho, including massage, singing and chanting, realigning his energies, a medicine ceremony, and political persuasion.

"Come," Deganawidah said to Hiawatha "you and I alone shall go first to the great wizard. I shall sing the Peace Song; you will explain the words of the law holding the wampum in your hand." By this time the beaded wampum had greatly increased in size and complexity, since it was the wampum of the Five Nations, encoding their councils of understanding, wisdom, insights, and practical solutions. "If we straighten his mind," Deganawidah continued, "the Longhouse will be completed and our work accomplished." We can imagine the careful preparations the two heroes made for this all-or-nothing encounter. The stakes had never been higher.

Entering their canoe, Deganawidah and Hiawatha began paddling across the lake. When they were about halfway across, they heard the voice of Tadadaho keening a fearsome chant, "*ASONKE-NE-E-E-E-EH?*" ("Is it not yet?").

"Ah," joked Hiawatha, "he is impatient for our message."

Almost immediately raging winds and waves, sent by Tadodaho as if in answer to his questioning cry, began to buffet the canoe. The wild elements were accompanied by the wizard's screaming declaration, "*ASONKE-NE-E-E-E-EH!*" ("It is not yet!")

But Deganawidah and Hiawatha, energized by zeal for their task, continued to paddle vigorously. Their dilemma affirms the sorry truth that when you set out on a course of action with the potential to change and reinvent your world and relationships, the waves of recalcitrance will often rise to impede your progress. It is then that you must not lose heart but renew your efforts and keep on going.

And so, battling forward, the pair soon landed the canoe and went to the wizard's lodge.

A key to this story is the irony that the wizard was both denying the possibility of change and, at the same time, impatient for it to happen ("Is it not yet?"). As soon as he expressed his impatience for transformation, his mind slammed down, and he answered his own question from the place of entropy ("It is not yet.") In our work all over the world, my associates and I find people as well as institutions who are in states of entropy, denying change, refusing opportunities. Yet even with these, we often catch, if only for the briefest moment, that gleam of "Is it possible? Is there really a way out? Is there a new order? Is there a new possibility for self, for society?" But then the need for the safety of what is known—even if what is known is terrible—reasserts itself, and it is back to basics, back to fundamentalisms, back to fortresses of "truth" and ancient but secure ideological havens. There is only one thing to do in such cases; you maintain a steadfastness of commitment and try to break through the entropy and stuckness by offering the fearful ones many surprises, many different ways of seeing and understanding their situation. I have been known to plunge conservative insurance executives in India into acting out on a personal level the life of Gandhi to help them recover a sense of service to their clients that exceeded their desire for material gain. I have also brought together Brahmin businessmen who had never known village life and simple villagers, who taught them a great deal more about the depth and beauty of their culture than they had previously realized.

In this spirit, Deganawidah and Hiawatha went to the wizard, and Deganawidah sang the Peace Hymn. As soon as he had finished the song, Deganawidah approached Tadodaho and began to soothe him by massaging his body with sacred herbs in a holy medicine ceremony designed to heal mind and body. There were witnesses to this process. In some tellings, the chiefs of the other tribes accompanied Deganawidah to Tadodaho; in others, it was the wizard's own people who witnessed his willingness to be soothed and massaged with sacred herbs.

Then, holding the strands of wampum which were by this point richly beaded with the contributions of the allies, Hiawatha said, "These are the words of the Great Law. On these words we shall build the House of Peace, the Longhouse, with five fires, that is yet one household. These are the words of Righteousness and Health and Power. These are the words of the renewal of ourselves and our society."

For a moment Tadodaho was drawn to the vision, but then he said, "No! No! What is this nonsense about houses and righteousness and health and power?"

Deganawidah responded, "The words we bring constitute the New Mind which is the will of the Holder of the Heavens. There shall be Righteousness when people desire justice, Health when people obey cooperative reason, and Power when people accept the Great Peace. These things shall be given form in the Longhouse, where five nations shall live in harmony as one family."

Then he said a remarkable thing, "At this very place, Tadodaho, where the chiefs of five nations shall assemble, I shall plant the Great Tree of Peace, and its roots shall extend to far places of the earth so that all humankind may have the shelter of the Great Law, the Great Peace."

Again Tadodaho was drawn to the vision, but then he retreated to his usual state of self-aggrandizement, saying,"What is that to me?"—in other words, "What's in it for me?"

Then Deganawidah spoke words to the effect of "You shall be of higher usefulness in this world." He said, "You yourself shall tend the council fire of the Five Nations, the fire that never dies." To be the Fire Keeper was essentially to be the chief sachem.

"And the smoke of that fire which you are tending shall reach the sky and be seen of all people"—in other words, we are offering you the opportunity to use your tremendous talents for a higher good.

For the two Peacemakers, it was not appropriate in their understanding to bring Tadodaho to justice or to punish him. Nor was it enough to persuade Tadodaho of the attractiveness of the Great Law of Peace or to pacify him with good medicine. No, the wizard had great skills, enormous energy, and the capacity to harness this energy, and the world needed this energy and this skill. But the Peacemakers' actions went far beyond mere pragmatism and a desire to use Tadodaho's skills, to the actual embodiment of a higher form of justice. For of what use is peacemaking if it requires retribution, and what is justice but peacemaking on a social scale? Even Hiawatha, who had been wounded beyond human endurance by the wizard, was willing not only to forgive but to work for the transformation and reempowerment of his former torturer. The Iroquois were then and continue to be a nation that knows that each individual is infinitely valuable regardless of his or her crooked actions or twisted paths. No effort is too great to bring such individuals to their spiritual reawakening.

Utterly startled by these words, Tadodaho said, "Where's the power to bring it to pass? How could that happen?" Then he began to howl, "*ASONKE-NE-E-E-E-EH.*" ("It is not yet.")

Whereupon Hiawatha and Deganawidah turned around, jumped into the canoe, and paddled away like mad. Deganawidah said, "Let's hurry, because this is the time. This is the open moment. We've got him now."

When they neared the middle of the lake, they heard Tadodaho's voice rush out to meet them. "*ASONKE-NE-E-E-E-EH!*" ("It is not yet.") The winds lifted the waves against their canoe, but they persisted in their efforts and soon reached the other shore. They signaled the assembled people from the tribes that had agreed to the Peace. The wizard's cry still ringing in their ears, they launched a flotilla of canoes and hastened back across the lake to reach the wizard's camp. All these people gathered before Tadodaho, as if to say, "You asked about the power to bring this to pass. Here is Power."

Bringing him forward, Deganawidah introduced Tadodaho to the assembled people. Perhaps Tadodaho looked less ferocious because he was reeling from the effects of Deganawidah's proposal that he serve instead of terrify. Deganawidah told Tadodaho that the people in front of him represented the nations who had subscribed to the new League.

Tadodaho asked, "All these people?"

"All these people. And, Tadodaho, they are willing to acknowledge you as preserver of their council fire."

Another chief spoke, indicating with a sweep of the hand the assembly, the warriors, and especially Jigonhsasee, the Peace Woman, the Mother of Nations, who also came forward: "These chiefs and this great woman, our mother, have all agreed to submit the Good News of Peace and Power to you. If you are able to approve and confirm this message, you will be the keeper of the fire of our confederate council. You will have a higher usefulness."

And in some versions of the story, the great Peace Woman, Jigonhsasee, spoke privately to Tadodaho. We cannot know what she said, but as the Mother of Nations, she must have provided a sense of new birth for Tadodaho, thus opening his New Mind. Hearing her secret nourishing words of regeneration, Tadodaho fell into utter silence.

And then Deganawidah said to him, "Behold, my friend! Here is the power. These are the Five Nations. Their strength is greater than your strength, but their voice can be your voice when you speak in council, and all people shall hear you. This shall be your strength in the future—not sorcery, but the will and creativity of a united people."

Tadodaho finally broke his silence and said, "It is well; I now truly confirm and accept your message."

Thus the mind of Tadodaho was at last made straight. Then Hiawatha, He Who Combs, combed the mattings, the twistings, the snakes out of the wizard's hair, and Deganawidah rubbed his body with wampum and herbs, with knowledge and with love. As Deganawidah massaged him, he straightened the seven crooks in Tadodaho's body, the crooks that had filled him with such hatred.

Many mythic traditions tell the story of the monster who is a powerful genius yet who hates and twists the world because he is so twisted. What is so deeply beautiful about this story is that, unlike many similar tales, here there is no battle done with the monster or dragon. Deganawidah and Hiawatha do not slay Tadodaho. Instead they heal him and enlist his help. The message seems to be that no face is so false that there is not truth within it, no life so twisted that it cannot be made straight.

Finally Deganawidah addressed Tadodaho in his state of New Mind and openness, straightened, combed, massaged, healed, and made whole: "The work is finished; your mind is made straight; your head is now combed; the seven crooks have been taken from your body. Now you too have the New Mind. You shall from this time preside over the council, and you shall strive in all ways to make reason and the peaceful mind prevail. Your voice shall be the voice of the Great Law; all people shall hear you and find peace."[1]

And with these final words the evil spirit left Tadodaho completely, and he bowed, "I accept your message, and I thank you."

Thus Deganawidah healed the wicked one, while Hiawatha combed the snakes from his hair. Together they invested the former monster with noble usefulness.

NOTES

[1] Many of the beautiful statements made by Deganawidah through-out this telling are drawn from *The White Roots of Peace* by Paul Wallace.

COMBING AND STRAIGHTENING THE LIES

TIME: Two hours.

MATERIALS: Pads or rugs for the floor.

MUSIC: Native American flute music.

INSTRUCTIONS FOR GOING SOLO: This process requires one other person.

We're embarking on a process of healing and truth-finding that can bring about the betterment of our minds, our bodies, and even our professions. In this book we have been seeking the bedrock of personal truth—physical, emotional, and mental. Knowledge of this truth brings courage to live as Peacemakers. Again, we will follow the events of the story of Deganawidah quite literally. We recall that Hiawatha, He Who Combs, combed the "snakes"—that is, the twisted, matted tangles of distorted thinking—out of Tadodaho's hair. Through a variety of means and ceremonies, including, perhaps, massage, Deganawidah straightened out the seven crooks of wickedness in the wizard's body. For our part, we will begin to heal the Tadodaho within ourselves and each other by employing a process that allows us to comb the energy fields around our partner's body while encouraging our partner to speak of the false beliefs that make him or her "crooked" and the great truths that will straighten out these twists and turnings.

We will perform what hypnotists refer to as "mesmeric passes" over the bodies of our partners. These passes, probably used for thousands of years by healers in traditional cultures, were redis- covered in the eighteenth century by a Viennese physician, Franz

Anton Mesmer. His use of these passes marked the beginnings of formal medical hypnosis. Dr. Mesmer found he could balance his patients' energy fields to allow for more rapid healing of a variety of physical and mental conditions. Mesmer gave the name "animal magnetism" to what he envisioned as a physical force or fluid which permeated the universe and to which the human nervous system is somehow akin. He believed that by having the healer channel this force through his or her hands as they made passes over the body, many imbalances could be corrected. In many cases, this process appeared to be of therapeutic benefit to the patients. No doubt many of these patients experienced deep hypnotic trances during and as a result of this procedure.

Although discredited in his own time, Mesmer's work has come to be revalued in the light of new findings concerning the depth of hypnotic trances that can be elicited by these measures. In trance states the local mind of daily worry releases its stranglehold on the body and allows the wisdom of the body to make its own way toward healing. Recent discoveries concerning the magnetic and bioelectric fields that surround the body have helped us understand why these passes are so effective. There is much in holistic and vibrational medicine, homeopathy, and acupuncture that suggest a certain validity to these yet unexplained methods.

In making the passes, following the example of Hiawatha's "combing," the hand of the healer does not touch the body; rather it moves slowly and gently, as well as respectfully through the energy fields that surround the body. As the body's fields are being combed, one can sense the mind-body field strengthening, relaxing, and opening to deeper knowings from within.

Many therapists have found this process very useful in their practice. It can be applied in other ways as well, to help worried or upset friends to relax, to sooth anxious or distraught family members or, as we will use it today, to discover deeper truths about our lives and work. In Part Two of the process, we will demonstrate the wider usefulness of this process as we move from personal healing and truth finding into discovering the deeper realities about our professions and community involvements.

SCRIPT FOR THE GUIDE:

PART ONE

We begin with "straightening" the twistings and distortions which almost every person tends to hold in the mind and body. We now know that nearly every mental belief has some physical corollary or embodiment.

Now, each one of us tends to hold both a Great Lie and a Great Truth in our being. Believing and acting out of our Great Lie can put crooks in our body and snaky twistings into our mind. By Great Lie we do not mean a deep, dark secret or a monstrous untruth that we have told. Rather, we mean beliefs about ourselves that have become habits of thinking that debilitate and inhibit our lives, even though they may no longer be true, or may never have been true. These lies need to be straightened out and untwisted in the mind and body.

Would each of you choose a partner, please. One partner will lie down, and the other will kneel at the side. The kneeling partner, who will be the healer, will take his or her dominant hand and hold it several inches above the partner's body. It is appropriate to ask permission to engage and work with your partner's field of energy. Also, clear extraneous thoughts from your mind, center your body, and send healing, caring energy to your hands. Then you will begin to run your hand down along your partner's body very slowly, using the fingers as combs to straighten and align the energies. You will start above the head and move down over the torso, then the legs, and off the feet. When I tell you to begin, you will practice the mesmeric passes for several minutes before you start to speak. Take the time to discover your own style of making the passes. For some they will be rapid; for others they will be very slow. Make sure that you feel a slight electrical tingle of connection. Your partner can even tell you when he or she feels that connection, which can be felt initially as a click or a joining of fields of energy between the two of you and can have both a soothing as well as an energizing effect.

After a few minutes, continuing to make the passes and combing the fields, you will ask your partner, "What is a Great Lie you have told about yourself that has caused you to feel twisted?" The partner will speak about some lie that he or she has continuously held or repeated.

After you have heard the lie and have combed it, you will say to your partner, "I, as Hiawatha, He/She Who Combs, now ask you what is the Deeper Truth, the True Face behind that False Face?" Here are several examples of this dialogue from Mystery School:

Woman participant: My Great Lie is that I cannot accept love from others, partly because I don't feel worthy. And also I tell myself the lie that I will have to do something to keep others loving me.

Partner (continuing to "comb" the fields): I, as Hiawatha, She Who Combs, now ask you what is the Deeper Truth, the True Face behind that False Face?

Woman participant: My truth is that I accept love all the time. Love is all around me, and I know it. And I don't have to do anything. Love has nothing to do with deserving. It's simply in the air that I breathe.

Another example of the dialogue went as follows:

Male participant: My Great Lie is that I no longer have enough energy or time to do the things that I think I want to do.

(After being asked for the Deeper Truth): My truth is that I always have energy and time to do the things that I truly want to do. My lie involves things that I really don't want to do anyway. My truth is that I can do what I want and find resources of time and energy to do those things that truly matter to me.

As you who are being combed realize and open to the Deeper Truth, you may feel that your bioelectrical fields, what are called the Life fields, are charging and energizing your Deeper Truth.

And you who are combing and healing should speak words to acknowledge this strengthening by saying words such as, "I, as He/She Who Combs, affirm that you have stated your Deeper Truth. And I comb a sense of clarity and straightness through your entire body."

Let us begin now. Please take the first few minutes of working together to establish the connection, as the healing partner combs the fields in a motion that starts at the top of the head and extends as far down the body as possible. Remember to keep the hand several inches above the body or at a distance at which you can easily feel the bioelectric fields of the body. After the hand has reached as far down as it can, swing it around outside the partner's energy fields and begin again from the top of the head. Bringing it back up the front of the body may "ruffle" the fields and break the connection. I will let you know when to begin asking your partner to tell you about the Great Lie. For now, just begin to comb the fields.

(After some three to five minutes during which the Guide has made sure the passes are being made effectively, she will say:) Now you who are taking the role of Hiawatha and recombing the fields, continue to do that as you ask your partner, "Tell me your Great Lies." The partner who is lying down and taking the role of Tadodaho should begin by speaking of one debilitating untruth he or she has held. When the partner has finished speaking, the Hiawatha should say, "I, as Hiawatha, He/She Who Combs, now ask you what is the Deeper Truth, the True Face behind that False Face?" When the partner has spoken the Deeper Truth, the Hiawatha will say words such as, "I, as He/She Who Combs, affirm that you have stated your Deeper Truth. And I comb a sense of clarity and straightness through your entire body."

As time permits, you may wish to speak several lies and truths in this manner. You have fifteen minutes of clock time to do this before the partners exchange roles. Begin. (Fifteen minutes)

(When the fifteen minutes are up the Guide will ask the partners to come to natural ending. Then advise them to stand up slowly and stretch, perhaps to dance a little, and to have a drink of water. The

Guide will then ask the partners to exchange roles and repeat the directions given above.)

Part Two

(After a short break the Guide will invite the entire group to gather together in the center of the room. The Guide will say:)

Now we will work to comb and straighten the lies that have hampered our work in our professional and social lives. Since the process we are doing is a healing, let us begin by healing the healers, including therapists, hospital workers, body workers, doctors and nurses, and anyone else who is connected with the healing professions. Would those of you who consider yourself to belong to this group please lie down together, with your heads in the same direction. The rest of the group should stand or kneel surrounding the group. We on the outside of this group of healing professionals will begin to comb and straighten the fields around this profession.

Now, I will ask you who are members of this group to raise your hand if you wish to tell a Great Lie that is associated with your profession or with the health care field in general. I, as Guide, will go to each person who has a hand up and ask the person to speak of such a lie. An example might be, "Hospitals are completely inhospitable places." After each has done so, I will say, "Now tell me the Deeper Truth." The person might say something like, "Every hospital can be a community of people interacting and being healed together."

As the people lying down speak these lies, the surrounding members of the group should comb and straighten the fields of life over these health care professionals. Please try to let your hands move together in one direction from their heads to their feet. (Five to ten minutes)

(After all the Great Lies and their Deeper Truths have been spoken and there are no more hands up of people who want to speak, the Guide will say:) We affirm that much of value has been spoken here and comb these truths into the energy fields of the health care profession so that those who are here can feel the twistings of their lies being straightened. Receive now the energy and passion and commitment to act to make positive changes in your profession. From this local field, we are generating change in the larger field. As Deganawidah forged the Iroquois Confederacy, so we forge a new confederacy of the spirit of health and of health-giving throughout the country and throughout the world.

Please affirm that this is so using the ceremonial words: "We take hold of it. We embrace it. We take hold of it. We embrace it."

(The Guide thanks the health care workers and invites them to stand up and join the other participants. Then the Guide invites another profession to come forward, such as educators. Here is an example directed to this group:)

Now, I would like those who are involved in education to lie down together, heads in the same direction as the previous group. Take a minute to look around you as you lie down, to see who the other members of your education clan are and to see who your allies are— those who will comb and straighten your lies and comb and infuse your body with your truths.

And would the rest of the participants surround them and begin combing out the twisted fields of this profession. Now, I will ask you educators to raise your hands and, as I come to you, to speak of a particular Great Lie that is associated with your profession or with the field of education in general, such as the lie that "children in inner-city settings cannot learn." Then, when I ask you to do so, speak the Deeper Truths about schools and education. For example, you might say, "There's no such thing as a stupid child; only stupid systems of education."

Raise your hand to indicate that you wish to speak your lie. Then when I ask you to speak your truth concerning education, please do so as your friends comb and straighten the field of education surrounding you.

(After all the lies and truths have been spoken, the Guide will say words that Empower the field of education, such as:) These Deeper Truths about education are moving in now through the fields of your life, giving you the courage to improve and enhance your profession. These truths are moving as well into the wider fields of education, straightening its crookedness, bringing in the new possibility of a system of education that calls forth the possible human in everyone.

Please affirm that this is so using the ceremonial words: "We take hold of it. We embrace it. We take hold of it. We embrace it."

(The Guide thanks the educators and invites them to stand up and join the other participants. Then the Guide invites other professions to come forward. The Guide will continue this process according to the makeup of the larger group. There might be groups having to do with artists and actors, government and business, spirituality, members of minorities, and people whose primary task is to raise families. Groups with similar aims can be blended together. The procedure for each group should follow the ones above, each sequence ending with an exhortation on the part of the Guide or others to take the Deeper Truths back into their lives and profession. It is wise to state as well that what is being done here moves out on waves of affirmation to enhance the profession throughout the community and beyond. The Guide should allow from five to ten minutes for each profession, depending on the size of the group. When all the groups have finished, the Guide might say:)

In the great story which we are following, Tadodaho was honored after the crooks had been combed out of his body and mind and he himself had come to accept the New Mind and the New Peace. He was made the keeper of the council fire, a central authority and an organizer of the ways of peace among the tribes of the confederacy. The story tells us he made a very good job of it, holding the council fire so that it continued to burn brightly. And down through the centuries, the keeper of the council fire, a member of Onondaga tribe, is still called the Tadodaho.

Much powerful energy is bound up in negative ways of being and thinking. Once we release it, it becomes a profound force for good, for engaging finer motivations and greater truths. We have combed the lies out of our personal lives as well as out of our professions and fields of endeavor. We have lit the council fire of Deep Truth about our way of perceiving and renewing these fields. Now let us go into the world and live it beautifully. Our true Tadodaho nature has been released and recognized as good and as useful for the greater good of all.

8

THE GREAT TREE OF PEACE

▲▲▲

At last, the League was formed. To mark the occasion, De-ganawidah gave a speech to the five tribes gathered now in peace. His words and the spirit of his words have been cherished in the memories of many generations of wampum keepers who have lived since that time—for at least five hundred years, perhaps more. His address included a form of constitution for the Five Nations of the Iroquois, one that, as we noted earlier, greatly influenced the founders of the American democracy and, years later, those statesmen seeking a model for the United Nations.

After establishing the possibility of a world of peace, Deganawidah and Hiawatha and their colleagues created a way of living in this new world and maintaining it. To this end, they devised a series of unforgettable symbols, potent images that would act to prime the peace continuously and keep it alive in the minds and hearts of the people. He and his colleagues also worked out the details of how the peace would be kept and who would be invited to participate in it. The most powerful symbols revolved around a tree. First, Deganawidah announced that he would plant a tree of the Great Long Leaves (designated by some as a white pine), which he named the Great Tree of Peace, whose four white roots of truth would spread through the world in the four cardinal directions, carrying news of the peace. These roots could be traced back to this source tree itself, he said, by any nation or people yearning for peace, consolation, and kinship. Even today the tradition welcomes any person wishing to learn the Law of the New Mind and take refuge in the branches of peace. Thus Deganawidah's Great Tree became a version of the *axis mundi*, the mythological tree which supports the world. The branches protected the members of the union, while the tree itself climbed up toward the Great Spirit, announcing to all that peace existed among humankind.

As he planted the tree, Deganawidah did a strange and powerful thing. He invited the warriors to bury their instruments of war under the tree, saying, "I now uproot this tree and command you to throw all of your weapons of war into the chasm to be carried by the undercurrents of water to the furthest depths of the earth. Now I place this tree back over this chasm, throwing away war between us forever and ensuring that peace shall prevail."[1] The symbolism of this act is clear: Along with their weapons, the warriors would throw away all thoughts of making war and the "Evil Mind" of hatred and enmity that fed them. From this action comes the expression "to bury the hatchet."

Above the Great Tree of Peace, Deganawidah envisioned an eagle, whose far-seeing eyes would be alert to the slightest sign of danger to the tree's roots and, thus, to peace. Like the ever-vigilant eagle, Deganawidah seemed to be saying, one cannot be lazy or mindless and embrace peace, for the peace he had worked to achieve was a vigorous passionate ideal, not an insipid state of passivity. The bonds of kinship and community which stretched through the tribes were designed to keep alliances strong. In strength and in the recognition of that strength, people would be free to live their lives without fear.

In what might be called his constitutional address, Deganawidah also urged the people to maintain friendships energetically. Strong human connections were essential to the vigor and strength of the Great Peace. Greet eagerly the stranger at the door, he said; make him or her a friend. A gracious and generous hospitality makes for a hospitable world. Evidence that this sense of fellow-feeling was lacking in the white world appalled the Indian, as did other examples of meanness of spirit. Typical was the shock of an Iroquois in the eighteenth century, who told Benjamin Franklin, "I don't understand you people. When a white man comes to my lodge and he is hungry and tired, I feed him, I give him nourishment, I try to make him well. But not long ago in your town of Albany I was hungry, and because I had none of your currency, I was called a 'lazy Indian,' and told to leave. I don't understand you people with lives based on currency." Like the Iroquois, indigenous people the world over react with sorrow and bewilderment when confronted with the arrogance and contempt of currency-fixated folk. There is a valuable lesson here for us: A culture based on money and possession of money debilitates caring and numbs our humanity.

Instead, Deganawidah's world centered itself on the well-being of all people. The sorrow of one became the sorrow of all, and the kinship and succor of all beings was regarded as the potential the Great Spirit had implanted in the human heart. In this spirit, Deganawidah urged people to let old insults and wrongs be forgotten. The peace that is within and the peace that is without cannot flourish when we spend all our time rehearsing our resentments, he said, for this will surely escalate to thoughts and actions of revenge. Peace becomes impossible when we expect others to make good on all our losses and dissolves into pathology and paranoia when we look on the other, be they person or nation, as the source of all betrayals. To replace such negative states of mind, Deganawidah urged the adoption of the condolence ceremony, the formal mourning of another's grief or pain which, when employed with subtlety and power, fostered sympathy and healing among and between all who grieved and all who witnessed the grieving.

The understanding that the League would be like the Longhouse implied that many things, such as hunting and fishing grounds, would be shared equally. This ideal of a shared earth is one of the greatest of Native legacies. Time and again the Indians reminded the Colonists that the earth who is our mother belongs to no one and is graciously available to all. Needless to say, this belief was taken by some European settlers as confirmation that the Natives were savages who lacked the civilized European person's understanding of property. Since they felt no pride in possessions, the Indians were soon considered less than human and treated as such, as the terrible decimation of both the Native peoples and their lands can testify. I remember talking to a Shoshone woman after a lumber company had illegally chain-sawed thousands of the great pine trees on her reservation—nature's work of millennia destroyed in a few days. "The white men are crazy," she said. "Don't they know that by killing the trees that way and without asking their permission, they are not only killing our Mother, the Earth, but are killing themselves?" For Deganawidah and the League, the world was a place where the finned, the crawlers, the wingeds, the burrowers, the four-leggeds, the two-leggeds, the plants, trees, rocks, forests, mountains, plains, waters, sun, moon, stars, earth and sky were kinned and consecrated, where nothing was held as separate in the sacred hoop of creation, and all was shared through the blessing of the Great Spirit. It was ecology in its essence, community in its most comprehensive form.

Freedom of speech and of religion were already so deeply a part of tribal life that they needed no expressed statement. Even people adopted into the tribes were expected to worship their own gods in their own way. Sad to say, the tradition of freedom of religion made the Indians especially vulnerable to Christian missionaries. Natives would tell the black-robed priests, "We have our own religion, but we're willing to hear about yours." When the missionaries insisted that their religion was the only true faith, the Indians were amazed, knowing that the Great Spirit was called by many names and had many faces and stories. The priests, however, were adamant. When they heard the story of Deganawidah, they would counter with such words as, "Ah, you know of a virgin birth and a savior, too? Well, yours is a false telling, the work of the Evil One. You've been living a lie. Now, we've got the real story, the only virgin birth and the only true Savior. You'd better follow our way or be damned forever." Here too, the subtleties of spirit of native folk once again fell victim to the absolutes of the European mind.

To empower and govern the Confederacy, Deganawidah established the Great Council. Representatives from each tribe would meet around the council fire, kept by Tadodaho. The council was to meet at least once a year. Though some tribes had more representatives among the total of fifty in the Great Council, each tribe had only one vote. Clear safeguards were placed on the leaders of the Council. They were to be the servants of their people, never their lords. Their job was to be generous, long-suffering, and sensitive, except in one way. Deganawidah advised the chiefs that their "skin should be seven thumbs thick so that no outrageous criticism or evil magic could pierce them." The leader was to maintain his or her center of truth, pray constantly to the Great Spirit for courage and clarity, and always think of the well-being of the people. That way, criticism or evil magic would only be a goad to greater service, an impetus to deeper commitment. How different this was from our present sorry scene in which criticism, the daily bread of any political leader, is so often met with elaborate defenses which attempt to throw the blame on others. How often have our governmental officials sought to cover up or deny some mistake or perceived error? The money, time, and energy spent in these cover-ups is exorbitant, a voracious worm gnawing at the innards of governance. Deganawidah's advice on this point was clear. "Listen to, but do not be affected by criticism," he said. "Respond to it wholesomely. Your job is to protect the law."

Deganawidah's new plan of governance also incorporated many intricate checks and balances, so that no one leader could claim autocratic power. The position of tribal chief was not dynastic; rather, the chief had to be seen and recognized over and over again as worthy of leadership. Furthermore, Deganawidah established the precedent that each tribe or clan would have two leaders—a principle one and his associate. The two worked together to assure the good of all. Since the title *sachem* means, as we have noted, "he does good" or "the good minds," a man had to be seen and known as one who did good in order to qualify for the role.

We recall, as well, that it was the clan mother who both selected and guided the sachem. Her choice, however, had to be ratified by both the consensus of the clan and the agreement of the chief's council of the nation. Should it happen that a sachem was not performing his role well, the clan mother tried to persuade him to better behavior. If that didn't work, the clan mother went to the clan elders and brought them into the discussion with the erring chief. If this was ineffective, she brought in other members of the society with other frames of mind to persuade or retrain him. They rarely gave up on anybody. Only if all these kinds of persuasion failed, did the clan mother actively and personally intervene. Only she could determine that a person was no longer fit to be chief. That decided, the clan mother would choose another chief, always guided by the understanding that governance involved preserving each human life and bringing it to its highest fulfillment. Efficiency was not an end; effectiveness in human terms was the supreme goal. Equal rights for women among the Iroquois were established in law by the power vested by Deganawidah in the clan mothers.

Deganawidah also provided the nation with a pattern for meetings of the yearly Great Council. Each opened with a prayer of thanksgiving to the earth and to all that was in it: "I thank you for the earth. I thank you for the waters. I thank you for the corn and for the harvest." Thanks were also given to a prodigious number of other particular things, events, and holy beings. I have attended Native ceremonies of thanksgiving where gratitude was expressed for so many particular things that it seemed nothing could have been left out. This tradition is a magnificent teaching: discussions and problems can be considered only after everyone is in an exhilaration of thanksgiving! And not even then, for next came songs to commemorate the founding of the League. Then came a kind of choral roll call of the tribes, with each acknowledging its attendance by song or chant. After all this, when they sat before the council fire, proposals were made with the use of wampum, and three kinds of debate were held for each issue: within a tribe, with a sister tribe, and then with the entire confederacy. In our terms, it would be like debating an issue within one's state, within one's bioregion, and then nationally. If discussion became stymied because of insoluble disagreements, the issue was sent back to the point in the process at which the debate had foundered. The Onondaga representative, as keeper of the fire, could break a tie vote or make a choice when two sides failed to agree.

In another wise decision, Deganawidah declared that the Great Council was to be adjourned when night fell, because overlong discussions might lead to raised tempers and thus become a threat to peace. Council debates knew no such thing as filibustering. An issue was not open to public debate on the day it was put before the council. Instead, everybody thought about an issue for a while after it was presented, and only then did they bring it up for discussion.

Another cherished tradition encouraged by Deganawidah and practiced by many tribes in the Americas was the use of the wampum strands as an aid to serious talking and deep listening. It was understood that when a speaker in council held the wampum, he or she would speak from his or her deepest truth and most essential knowing. By tradition, others weren't allowed to jump up to make their points. Instead, they were to attend fully to what was being said as the belt of wampum passed from speaker to speaker. "Deepen the issue" was the spoken and unspoken guidance. Imagine how it would be if the presiding officer of the Senate were to say, "Will the Junior Senator from Vermont please rise and deepen the issue that the Senior Senator from Minnesota has just raised?"

Benjamin Franklin, who observed at first hand the workings of the Haundenosaunee government, had this to say about the conducting of council meetings:

> He that would speak, rises. The rest observe a profound Silence. When he has finished and sits down, they leave him five or six minutes to recollect, that he has omitted anything he intended to say, or has any thing to add, he may rise again and deliver it. To interrupt another, even in common Conversation, is reckoned highly indecent. How different it is from the conduct of a polite British House of Commons, where scarce a Day passes without some Confusion that makes the Speaker hoarse in calling to order and how different from the mode of Conversation in many polite Companies of Europe, where if you do not deliver your Sentence with great Rapidity, you are cut off in the middle of it by the impatient Loquacity of those you converse with, & never suffer'd to finish it.[2]

When a decision was reached in the Great Council, the Onondagas, the fire keepers and home tribe of the meeting place for the Council, received the final report and made a formal announcement of the national decision.

Deganawidah also presented the people with numerous symbols to be used at council meetings to encode the principles of the Great Peace in tangible ways. Most important was the above-mentioned wampum belts (the nation's "heart" according to one elder), which carried the full story of the people, their history and actions, and served as a kind of hieroglyphic representation of the nation's belief systems. A white wampum mat, symbol of purity and peace, was to be spread before the chiefs meeting in council. A feathered wing was provided to sweep away confusion ("dirt") or anger from the white wampum mat. A special stick was designated to lift away any encroaching "insect" or "animal" seen to endanger the children even unto the seventh generation. Thus the future was always alive. No decision was made without considering its effect on the generations to come. (This custom is similar to the "Children's Fire" placed at the center of the Medicine Wheel, a symbolic form used by other Native American tribes to encourage discussion and insight.) The council fire itself was never allowed to die. The chiefs, however, were enjoined not to spend their time "blowing ashes" at each other, which meant creating mischief and thereby weakening their authority and the people's faith in them and in the union. Deganawidah also placed deer antlers, with their symbolism of many branches coming from the one, on the heads of the chiefs as a sign of their authority. The antlers were also believed to hold a kind of spiritual power, which made the chief more receptive to what was going on. Today we might think of them as antennae, picking up the news from the universe.

In addition to the Longhouse, the Tree of Peace, the watchful eagle, and the objects for use by the Great Council, Deganawidah offered another striking symbol to strengthen the sense of union in his people's minds. He took an arrow and broke it. Then he took an arrow from each tribe and bound them together. He tried to break them, but the the bound-together arrows could not be broken. The meaning was clear: In separation was weakness; in union, strength.

This glyph of bound-together arrows was later copied by the thirteen colonies to suggest the strength of their union. We see it today on our dimes and dollar bills and in many of our symbolic insignia, along with the watchful eagle and the leaves of the pine tree.

A further powerful bond among the nations was the clan system. Within each tribe were several clans: Turtle, Wolf, Deer, Hawk, Heron, Eel, Sandpiper, Snipe, and Big Bear, Younger Bear, and Suckling Bear (papa bear, mama bear, and baby bear). Each tribe within the confederacy had members belonging to several of these clans. In this way, an individual was related both within the tribe and across tribal lines. A Wolf person in the Mohawk tribe, for example, would have a kind of brotherhood or sisterhood with a Wolf person in the Seneca or Oneida tribes; a Sandpiper in the Cayuga would have a familial bond with an Onondaga Sandpiper. So in addition to his or her tribal identify, an individual had a kind of esoteric spiritual totemic identity. One was thus literally related to many people in other tribes and connected by ritualistic and blood ties from the mothers in potent and almost unbreakable ways.

Each succeeding chief or sachem of a particular tribe carried the name of the originals. So there was always a "Tadodaho" and a "Hiawatha," as well as a title that came down from the names of each of the fifty original delegates. This too provided symbolic structure. In fact, the protocol of the U.S. Senate borrows from this tradition in that senators are never addressed by name but rather as the Junior Senator from this state or the Senior Senator from that state. However, this seems a very bland version of the original intention. I wonder if our government leaders would act any differently if the President were always called the "George Washington" and the Vice President, the "John Adams"? What if being elected President meant that a person lost his or her local name altogether and took on an archetypal name? "Mr. Jefferson." "Mr Madison." It's a compelling idea to be reenergized with an archetypal name. There was, however, one exception to this tradition and that was Deganawidah himself. He declared that there was to be only one of him, so his name is rarely even spoken among his people. Instead they call him the Peacemaker or the Man from the North.

Finally Deganawidah enjoined the first chiefs not to think of themselves in carrying out their work, or even of their own generation, but to think always of the generations to come. He made provision for other nations to join the peaceful confederacy. The Tuscarora, in fact, later became the sixth nation to join the League. Others maintained respectful ties. But Deganawidah also made provision for an unhappy future. He urged the chiefs to think carefully about where danger could come from or how the Great Tree of Peace could be uprooted. He counseled them that if such danger could not be avoided, the leaders were to travel forth until they found a swamp elm and then bring their people to shelter within its branches. It was very important that at least a remnant of the peace-loving confederacy survive in a sheltered and protected place.

With these last admonitions given, Deganawidah declared that his work was finished. In some versions of the story, he then covered himself with elm bark and asked to be lowered into the ground to enter the womb of his great mother. From his place in the ground, he said, he would be able to hear how his Longhouse was being maintained. In other tellings of the story, he left by simply paddling away to someplace else. "It is time to go so that you are not dependent upon me," he said. Longfellow's story of Hiawatha also ends with the hero paddling away. Remember that Deganawidah had told his mother and grandmother, "If I have died and my work has failed, the tree will give blood when you strike it with your hatchet." While there is no record of the actual place or time of Deganawidah's death, the story tells us that the sentinel tree observed by his mother and grandmother lives on and has never given blood. As it is said of King Arthur, the legend of Deganawidah has it that if he is ever needed or the peace should fail, his people should speak his name to the bushes and trees, and he will return. Among the tribes of New York state there is the sense now that Deganawidah is being called and will soon return. Certainly his story is rising again, and he is returning through that story.

Deganawidah's work lives on, as Jack Weatherford so elegantly reminds us in his concluding statement of his book, *Native Roots:*

The story was already an ancient one when the first settlers came from Europe, and the native people shared their knowledge of the Good Mind with the newcomers. The new people came to live under the Great Tree of Peace, but they did not know its history. They did not know of the weapons buried in the earth, or of the white roots of peace that needed to be watered and nourished to help the tree grow.

In the bountiful life we have been given in America, we have not always remembered the law of the Good (New) Mind. Sometimes we have reached out and taken an unfair share of the fruits of the tree. Sometimes we have enjoyed our place in the shade, but have not wanted to welcome others still suffering in the heat. Sometimes we have fouled the earth around the tree. We have spoiled the air and contaminated the water. In ignorance we have even hacked at the roots of the great tree. But the tree has survived.

The great pine tree of peace is now more than half a millennium old. Some of the centuries have been harsh ones, but the tree has weathered the struggles between natives and settlers, an evil era of slavery, a bloody civil war, and heavy losses in foreign wars. Despite the hardships and cruelties of American history, the roots of that great tree have continued to grow, and new nations have found shelter under its branches.

The tree offered sanctuary to people of all cultures looking for a better life in a new world, to people fleeing from war, tyranny, poverty, possession, famine, persecution and genocide. The newcomers often had no water to give the white roots other than their own sweat, tears and sometimes even blood. When they came without nourishment for the tree, the tree lived on their dreams and hopes, and it continued to grow.

We are the inheritors of a great American legacy: we are the children of Deganawidah. We are the children of Africa, Asia, Europe, the South Pacific, and all of the Americas, who have come to live under the peace of the great tree. We are the people who must uphold the Good Mind that our children may inherit this legacy of righteousness, health and spiritual power. We are the people who now must nurture the Great Tree and water its white roots of peace.[3]

All of us are new seedlings sprung from this tree. In a world that is quickly moving toward a planetary civilization composed of many different cultures, it is essential that we send the white roots of peace all over the world. Perhaps it is for this reason that the Great Spirit has helped encourage the rise of this story again from the soil of America. This tale is a great rooted blossomer, rapidly growing and greening, reaching across time and space to give us guidance, protection, and peace.

I believe the legend of Deganawidah to be one of the deepest and most potent stories to come out of America. I hope many of you who read this book will use this story, whether you are teachers or counselors, artists, writers, health and care givers, business folk, professionals, or white collar workers, those who work in factories, or those who do the holy work of bringing up families. Above all, tell this story to your neighbors and your children; tell your old and new friends that the Great Tree of Peace is now spreading its roots to embrace the whole planet and that the Peacemaker has returned to dwell in the lake of our hearts.

And so, for our final act in this Manual for the Peacemaker, let us go about celebrating the time of the new greening and planting our own white pine of peace in the world in which we live.

NOTES

[1] Quoted by Oren Lyons in "Land of the Free, Home of the Brave," in *Indian Roots of American Democracy*, ed. Jose Barreiro, p. 33.

[2] "Remarks Concerning the Savages of North-America," *Benjamin Franklin: Writings*, edited by J. A. Leo Lemay (New York: The Library of America, 1987), pp. 970–1.

[3] Jack Weatherford, *Native Roots: How the Indians Nourished America* (New York: Crown, 1991), p. 287.

A FESTIVAL OF CELEBRATION/ PLANTING THE GREAT TREE OF PEACE

TIME: Three hours or more. If planting the Tree of Peace is to be done outdoors, it is recommended that this process be during the daytime.

MATERIALS: Drum and rattles. Dried sage leaves and/or smudge sticks. Tapes of Native American songs, although it would be wonderful if there are those among you who know some songs and can teach them to the others. A large candle. Paper, scissors, and markers or crayons to make hatchets. A small pine tree for planting, preferably a white pine, and a place outdoors where it can be planted. If the tree cannot be planted outdoors because of the weather, it can be planted in a very large pot, watered carefully, and replanted outdoors when that becomes feasible.

If possible, decorate the room with Native American crafts and symbols, making sure that each participant understands the meaning of each symbol. We are not "playing Indian" here. We are exploring and honoring traditions and ceremonials that come from the original inhabitants of North America, and the more we know about each tradition, the better it will be for all. Books that deal with Native symbols and traditions are to be found in the bibliography.

MUSIC: Native American songs and dances.

INSTRUCTIONS FOR GOING SOLO: This entire process can be done alone, following the instructions. However, it would be best if you could find one or more others to join you in this celebration. Put the dream induction on tape, and write in your journal whatever ideas you have about its interpretation.

Our journey with the Peacemaker concludes with a celebration that incorporates a number of aspects of Native American ritual tradition drawn from the ceremonies of many different tribes in which I and my associates have participated. They are not meant to be regarded as actual recreations of these ceremonies, for such can only be done by Native Americans themselves or by those who have walked a long way on the Native path and have received permission to offer the sacred ceremonies. In fact, if possible, the group that is taking part in the Manual for the Peacemaker should consider inviting a Native American to direct some part of the closing ceremonial, using his or her own traditions or adapting the ones found below. The planting of the Great Tree of Peace, however, is one ceremony that should be retained.

In the version of the story of the Peacemaker which took place during a weekend at Mystery School, we were fortunate to have with us Loretta Afraid-of-Bear Cook, a member of the Oglala Sioux tribe who is married to a Mohawk. She led us in a series of Mohawk processional songs and dances and then performed a very beautiful pipe ceremony. Since she is a "holder of the pipe," she has permission to perform those rites.

The spiritual genius to be found among many Native American peoples derives not only from a close contact with nature but also from rigorous participation in rites and ceremonies of extraordinary depth and meaning. These rites and ceremonies, many related to seasonal cycles, help participants understand the great patterns and innate values reflected in the mirror of nature and also intensify the experience of spiritual presence necessary to support a life oriented toward the sacred.

We who live under largely European and Middle Eastern religious and political dictates assent to certain expected behaviors as defined by law and commandments, but the Native American agrees to the Great Order by virtue of becoming a part of it ritually and thus by knowing it deeply from the inside as a spiritual participant. In this way, the will and intention of the individual becomes consonant with the will and intention of spirit and nature. To achieve this ceremonially, ritual actions must involve a complete immersion that engages the totality of who one is. Prayers and dances, purification in a Sweat Lodge, tests and challenges, vision quests, singing, and collective dreaming are but a few of the activities that bring one into alignment with nature and the Great Spirit.

The process that follows cannot accomplish this ritual alignment in its totality. Rather, the activities explained below reflect a typical festival night at Mystery School cast in the Native American tradition. If enacted in the proper spirit of reverence, however, these ceremonies can bring one to a clearer sense of the beauty and power of the originals. Please keep in mind, however, that it is not our intention here to follow the Iroquois model or, indeed, any particular tribal tradition. Tribal traditions are sacred to specific tribes and should remain so.

We begin, as many Native American ceremonies begin, by cleansing both the area and the participants with the holy smoke of burning sage leaves or a smudge stick. This action reminds the participants to cleanse themselves of negative thoughts and purifies the area of energies that are not helpful to the ceremonial. It is particularly important that one does not enter into sacred time or place holding grudges or resentments.

With the cleansing and purifying accomplished, we enter into the dance. For the Native Americans of virtually all the 485 tribes, dancing is the breath of life made visible. In dance, spirit and flesh are unified—the spirit is made flesh, and the flesh, inspirited. To move closer to the centers of power in nature, Native Americans often become in their dancing the things of the natural world, which then invest the dancer with their strength, power, and wisdom. Participants receive power through the songs and in the dance are able to touch those unknown and unseen elements which they sense in the world around them. Everything in Native life has its extension and counterpart in sacred dance. Indeed sacred dance might seem to be the extended archetypal reality made visible as the witness of the Great Spirit in everyday life. Thus there are dances for war, for peace, for victory, for joy, and for sorrow. There are dances for courtship, for marriage, and for fertility. There are dances and rituals devoted to bringing rain, especially among the agricultural peoples of the southwest. The animal dances of the hunting people and the fish dances of the fishing people give the dancers a sense of identity and communion with their relatives, the four-legged and the finned, so that killing can be acknowledged in sacred time and space, and the people eat sacramentally only what they need.

The costumes and paraphernalia of the dances are extremely complex and require considerable preparations for their creation and maintenance. By contrast, the dance steps themselves, although powerful and very ancient, are relatively simple as compared to the complexities of the ballet or of Hindu or Balinese dances. Native dances are relaxed, and their steps are executed with an inner grace and simplicity that demands a deep involvement of the dancer in the dance. The dancer must also maintain a balance in his or her mind between alert consciousness and trance, especially during ceremonies such as the Long Dance which goes on all night.

Unique to Indian dance are steps that favor bent knees with the body in an erect and straight posture. Unlike African dances, the torso does not move much. Nor is there any complex use of the arms as there are among dancers of India and Bali, except when the dancer is performing a mimetic dance representing animals or birds. There are male dances, female dances, and some dances involving both men and women. Native American women sometimes dance in curious steps which look a bit like the old Charleston but are performed to traditional drumming. Nowadays, different tribes are learning each other's dances; recently I saw a wonderful performance of the dances of the Plains Indians by Iroquois dancers of the Buffalo region of New York.

Our dancing will be followed by collective dreaming, an activity that recalls the midwinter ceremony of the Iroquois, a powerful therapeutic activity in which dreams are interpreted and the wishes that appear in the dream are actualized for the benefit of the dreamer.

The next ceremony is the Sacred Hoop of All Beings. At the end of many Native meetings or ceremonials, the participants recite a phrase given here in the Lakota language, *"Mitakuye Oyasin,"* which means "All my relations" or "We are all related." The phrase recalls the Native knowing that any activity of Native life—cooking, planting, hunting, dancing—is dynamically and powerfully inter-connected with everything else. Everything is in relationship or in a series of relationships that reach further and further out: relationships within the immediate family reaching out to the extended family, and outward again to the clan and to the tribal group. Relationships do not stop there but extend out to embrace and relate to the environment: to the land, the animals, the plants, the clouds, the elements, the waters, the heavens, the stars and, ultimately, to the entire universe. This belief in the power of relationship is deeply reflected in key Native symbols, especially the Sacred Hoop that includes all beings and all things.

In his conversations with John Neihardt in 1931, Black Elk complained that Indians were forced to live in square log houses, a form without power. He said:

You have noticed that everything an Indian does is in a circle, and that is because the Power of the World always works in circles, and everything tries to be round. In the old days when we were a strong and happy people, all our power came to us from the sacred hoop of the nations, and so long as the hoop was unbroken, the people flourished. The flowering tree was the living center of the hoop and the circle of the four quarters nourished it. The east gave peace and light, the south gave warmth, the west gave rain, and the north with its cold and mighty wind gave strength and endurance. This knowledge came to us from the other world with our religion. Everything the power of the World does is done in a circle. The sky is round, and I have heard that the earth is round like a ball, and so are all the stars. The wind, in its greatest power, whirls. Birds make their nests in circles, for theirs is the same religion as ours. The sun comes forth and goes down in a circle. The moon does the same, and both are round. Even the seasons form a great circle in their changing, and always come back again to where they were. The life of man is a circle from childhood to childhood, and so it is in everything where power moves. Our teepees were round like the nests of birds, and these were always set in a circle, the nation's hoop, a nest of many nests, where the Great Spirit meant for us to hatch our children.[1]

On another occasion in 1948, Joseph Epes Brown asked Black Elk how he, in his late eighties, could crawl around on the floor, relating to a very young child. Black Elk replied with the image of circularity: "I who am an old man about to return to the Great Mysterious [*Wakan Tanka* in Lakota] and a young child is a being who has just come from the Great Mysterious; so it is that we are close together."[2]

In our ritual, we will engage in a ceremony of calling in the Sacred Hoop of all Beings. We each will speak for one or more members of the sacred Hoop—animals, plants, people, and other parts of creation. In so doing, we remind ourselves of the great Nest of nests that the Creator has given us and which we have it in our power through speech and consciousness to express and appreciate.

We will conclude our journey through the Manual for the Peacemaker with a ceremony of burying our hatchets of war and negativity under a white pine tree which we will plant and water with our most beautiful intentions. We will close with a chanting of the Beautyway of the Navaho and go back into the world as Peacemakers and tellers of this great story.

SCRIPT FOR THE GUIDE:

PART ONE: CLEARING THE ENERGY/BRINGING HOLY SMOKE TO THE SPACE AND THE PEOPLE

Would you all please stand in a circle. We begin now as do the Native Americans of many traditions by purging with Holy Smoke all negative thoughts held, given, or received by anyone here. (The Guide makes her way around the circle carrying a smoking smudge stick, sweetgrass stick, or burning sage leaves in a nonflammable container like a large shell. The Guide brushes the smoke down the sides, front, and back of each person. In some Native traditions, one uses a feather to gather the smoke around each person. As the Guide does this, she says:) As you are purified with this smoke, know that our brothers and sisters among the Native tribes of this land believe that this ceremony puts all bad thoughts or vibrations into their place or gives one a better understanding of them. (Note to the Guide: It is important to smudge not just the people but the room as well, thereby purifying the space in which this ceremony is to take place. Thus you should also sweep the room with the smoke.)

PART TWO: INVOKING THE POWERS OF THE DIRECTIONS

(This ritual varies widely from tradition to tradition. The version given here is one we use in Mystery School, but the Guide can change it according to her preference.

The Guide invites all to face East and says:) We call upon the Powers of the East. The East is the place of beginnings, the place of the dawn, and of the spring; the place where the sun rises to illumine the earth. It is the place of the butterfly and eagle, the place of seeing wide and seeing clearly, of new birth. Everything rises and starts in the East. Everything is born in the East. Powers of the East, be here with us now.

(The Guide invites all to face South and says:) We call upon the Powers of the South, the place of the summer sun high and hot at noon, greening the summer grasses for our food. It is the place of flowers and fruits and all growing things. It is the place of warmth and heartfulness, of nurturance and endurance. Powers of the South help us to walk the good red road in right relations with all those we meet. Help us to remember Mouse and its loving attention to all details. Help us to remember laughter and Coyote who brings us people to teach us the lessons we need to learn in this life. Help us to walk as the child in pure heart and heartfulness. Powers of the South, be here with us now.

(The Guide invites all to face West and says:) We call upon the Powers of the West, the place of the autumn and of the dusk, the harvest, the reaping, and gleaning of our lives, the cutting away of all that no longer serves us with the black obsidian knife. The place that holds all the waters that cleanse, dissolve all impurities, and heal us. It is the place of Raven and of her magic, of the twilight—the two-light time, the place of introspection, of Bear climbing into the cave of the dreamtime, the looking-within place. Powers of the West, be here with us now.

(The Guide invites all to face North and says:) We call upon the Powers of the North, the place of the winter and the night, where the white mantle of wisdom covers the earth. The place of silence, of stillness, of the vastness of the sky and the air, of cool winds, and the silence of owl flight in the dark. The place where we have no attachment to the results of our actions or creations; the place of our ancestors; the place of the great archetypal beings—of white buffalo who reminds us of the ancient wisdom that lives in us all always. Powers of the North, be here with us now.

(The Guide invites all to look above and says:) To the Above—shine down your grace on us.

(The Guide invites all to look below and says:) To the Below—grant us your deepening powers so that we take our place on the Sacred Hoop.

(The Guide invites all to look within and says:) To the Great Powers within—know that within us is the place where all the Powers meet, and that the Sacred Hoop is within us—that each one can say, "I the hoop." Ho!

Part Three: The Dance

(The Guide invites the participants to form a circle for a Native American circle stepping dance. Several participants who are in the circle can accompany the dance with drumming and rattling, or the Guide may do the drumming. As the drum begins to sound a steady beat, the participants step around the circle. Facing inward, they step on their left foot, and then bring their right foot next to it and step on it. Continuing to do this, they dance around the circle, making several full revolutions of the circle so as to create the hoop. In this way they begin to dance the Great Circle of Life, embodying by dancing the powers of the directions which have just been invoked.

Participants who know simple songs from the Native tradition can sing them to the accompaniment of drum and rattle. A song that we use at Mystery School which honors the earth and our relation to the sacred hoop goes:

> The Earth is our Mother, we must take care of her.
> The Earth is our Mother, we must take care of her.

> HE YAHNE HO YAHNE HE YAHNA
> HE YAHNE HO YAHNE HE YAHNA

> Her Sacred Ground we walk upon, with every step we take.
> Her Sacred Ground we walk upon, with every step we take.

> HE YAHNE HO YAHNE HE YAHNA
> HE YAHNE HO YAHNE HE YAHNA

(The song is repeated throughout the circle dance. The Guide determines when the end of the dance should be and stops the drum.)

PART FOUR: THE DREAMING

(The Guide will say:) The Iroquois Midwinter Festival held in February to celebrate the new sun often included a ceremony of clan dreaming. During this process whoever had a dream came forward and enacted the dream. Then it was the job of others to guess the meaning of the dream. Whatever was guessed and seemed to be appropriate had to be done for the dreamer. For example, if a woman dreamed of acquiring land, she might lie down with a hoe by her side. The others might guess her need and allocate to her five furrows of corn land which she would be expected to plant and bring to harvest. The Iroquois believed that what we call the unconscious was powerful and spoke through dreams to tell people of the deep needs of their inner spirit. The community respected these needs and realized that continuing health could only be achieved by fulfilling them.

Now if you dream about acquiring real estate in mid-Manhattan, we can't help you realize your dream exactly. Nor can we help manifest your dream if it indicates you have designs on some other person. But what we can do is create a reasonable equivalent by suggesting an interpretation, one that speaks to the depth of one's yearning and offer plans for its fulfillment. In some cases, we may even be able to help manifest the desire in the dream. Of course, not everyone, perhaps only one or two of you, will have a dream which indicates a wish or a need. However, we will all do our best to help interpret the deeper meaning or the essential need that is contained in the dream.

(If the group is large, the Guide may want to divide it into smaller dreaming and interpretation groups, each constituting a kind of Longhouse. Then she says:)

I am now going to set up a Dreamtime—a very short period of clock time, about five minutes, which in dreamtime will be equal subjectively to all the time you need. For some it may seem to be hours or even days of dreaming; for others, no time at all. It may be that not everyone will dream. But some of you will, and we invite you to dream about a new time and a new possibility. So let us begin.

Please sit or lie down and close your eyes. Begin by following your breath all the way in and all the way out . . . Following your breathing all the way in and all the way out . . . Following your breathing all the way in and all the way out . . . Just following your own breathing . . .

You find yourself at the edge of a primal forest. And you wander in the forest. You wander past tall trees of many varieties. Past ancient oak trees, maple, chestnuts, birch. Past elm trees with their bark shagging off. Underfoot there's a thick matting of pine needles, of acorns, of pine cones, of ferns, of mushrooms. The sun dapples on and off as you walk through this thick forest. And as you walk you find yourself passing into an altered state.

And in that altered state it seems that you are in two realities: one the state in which you are walking and the other the state of the dream. And in the dream you find yourself dreaming.

And you dream that you find yourself at the edge of a great primal forest. And you step into that forest, thick with pine trees of all varieties, of giant oaks, of elm trees with shaggy bark. Walking on a thick, thick matting of pine needles, acorns, pine cones, fern, and fungus. The sweet resinous smell of the forest rising up to meet you with every footfall.

And you find yourself passing into yet a deeper and deeper inward state of consciousness. And yet you are aware of still walking. And in this inward state of consciousness you find yourself dreaming.

And you dream that you find yourself on the edge of a great primal forest. And you enter this primal forest, which is filled with pine trees of many varieties, of ancient tall oaks, of elm trees with shaggy bark. The sun dappling on and off through the thick, thick forest treetops. Underneath a thick, thick matting of pine needles, of pine cones and acorns, of ferns and fungus. Rich forest-sweet resinous smells rising up to your nose. And you find yourself dreaming.

And you dream that you're entering a primal forest. And you're walking into that forest. Walking past great pine trees of many varieties. Past ancient oaks. Past elm trees with shagging bark. The sun dappling on and off above the crowded treetops. Underneath a thick matting of pine needles, pine cones and acorns, ferns and mushrooms. And you see a great tree that seems to have an entrance in it, an ancient oak. An entrance or an open space. And you crawl into that open space. And you find that it leads to an underground cavern. And in that cavern you see a bed of pine needles. And the bed of pine needles is the Place of Dreaming. And it is the dreaming about the New Time, the New Possibility, perhaps, even, the New Peace.

And you lie down on that bed of pine needles in this cavern underneath the giant oak within this primal forest. And you begin to dream. And it is a dream that speaks to the New Time, to who and what you really are and what you need, that speaks to the present condition of time, of history, of humanity, of the planet. But it may speak uniquely to you.

And in the next five minutes or so of clock time, equal subjectively to all the time you need, you will dream the dream of the New Time as it pertains to you with your own symbols, your own meaning.

And now dreaming the dream, beginning NOW.

(After about five minutes, the Guide will say:) Now holding the dream, come up to full waking consciousness as I count from one to twenty.

Holding the dream. One, two. Arising from that bed of pine needles. Three, four, Ascending up the cavern. Five, six. Into the tree trunk. Seven, eight. Going out of the tree trunk. Nine, ten. Moving through the forest. Eleven, twelve, thirteen, fourteen. Past the pines, the oaks, the thick matting of pine needles, acorns, pine cones, mushrooms, ferns. Fifteen, sixteen. Out to the edge of the forest. Breathing deeply. Seventeen. Coming up to full waking consciousness. Eighteen, nineteen, twenty. Breathing deeply and stretching.

All right. Now let one who has had a dream and who asks for interpretation tell the dream. Not everyone may have had a dream and not every dream may need to be interpreted. But let one who has had a dream that needs to be enacted come forward.

(The Guide selects one person and says:) Now, tell your dream, but tell it in such a way that it can be enacted. Remember, the Iroquois did not speak the dream. People who are close to nature do not just speak dreams. They become them. You could do it almost as a charade.

And others will watch and listen deeply. And then they will offer interpretations and guidance as to the meaning and fulfillment of the dream.

(The Guide will allow from fifteen minutes to an hour or more, depending on the number of dreamers. After various speakers have given their interpretation, the Guide will assist the group in helping the dreamer discover what action he or she might take to fulfill the message of the dream.)

PART FIVE: SPEAKING WORDS
OF THANKSGIVING TO EACH OTHER

(The Guide says:) Would you offer, as the Iroquois people offered, brief words of thanksgiving and appreciation to each other, stating what you are grateful for. You may, for example, be grateful for something that others in the group helped you with in your dream or for something else they have done or been for you during this long journey we have taken together. In Mystery School, for example, people said things like the following to each other or to the group as a whole:

Female participant: Thank you for showing me that wild animals cannot be domesticated, should not be domesticated. That it's not their nature.

Male participant: You've rescued me on many levels. Not just in the dream, but in my life, through your style and your presence. Thank you very much.

Now please give thanks and appreciation to each other. (Five to ten minutes)

PART SIX: SPEAKING FOR THE
THE SACRED HOOP OF ALL BEINGS[3]

(The Guide says:) In our collective dreaming we may have found that new patterns of possibility have started to come forth. This is happening the world over as we enter more and more into planetary community life. A new and deeper story is emerging, not only between people and cultures but among all the things of the earth as well.

Aided by the media and the breaking down of traditional divisions between peoples and nations, there is a bleed-through all over the world of the dreaming—of the collective unconscious. We seem to be growing closer to what Teilhard de Chardin referred to as the Noosphere, the field of mind and soul that joins us all together. This field of mind is similar to what the aboriginal peoples of Australia refer to as the Dreamtime. It would appear that in some way the members of other species are joining us there too, or perhaps we are becoming conscious that they were there all the time. Let us now begin to celebrate this joining in a calling of the Sacred Hoop of All Beings.

But first, we must remember that Native American languages are very unlike ours. In our speech, a word is a symbol for meaning. In most Native languages, a word and its sound contain power, and word and meaning are one dynamic event. Sacred potency is therefore inherent in the sounding of words. To speak the name of anything is to evoke the powers inherent in that thing. That is why so many animal names are given to people. To be called "Mad Bear" is to evoke the fine fury of the raging bear each time one is called. Moreover, Native people deeply honor the fact that breath, which is associated with the life force, is the vehicle through which we create words. Words, born of breath, spoken in a sacred manner can embody the Great Spirit in the world. The sacred utterance of a word gives you power to be in touch not only with your own center and life force but with all the realms of being in the Sacred Hoop of the Great Spirit. So, as we begin to speak for each species or member of earth's great community, we will let ourselves be filled with the presence and spirit of the animal or plant for which we are speaking.

(The Guide brings a large candle into the center, lights it, and asks everyone to gather around it. Then she says:) If you would, now, look into that flame. And as you do, you will begin to feel yourself open to receiving the essence of some other species or part of the earth. When you have become conscious of such embodiment, you will speak, in sacred utterance, the dream of another species. Someone, for example, might speak for the whales or be inspired by some plant or element, rock or bird, and be moved speak for them.

Here are some examples of such speakings from the ceremony at Mystery School:

I speak for the dogs. Friends, allies, heart's companions that walk a piece of the road with you. Always there, without judgment, and yet wise. Deep friends. Transitional beings many of them, in a state of yearning. Great partners.

I speak for the milkweed pod. The seeds that grow so tightly and are so surrounded and so nurtured. And then burst forth in their time. And they fly and go to new places, and they seed whole new universes.

I speak for the rocks, for the minerals. God sleeps in the rocks. The bedrock under our feet is our mother.

I speak for the insects. Tiny little angels of the air that orchestrate symphonies to our sleeping subconscious when we dance in the grass as eternal children.

I speak for the seaweed embracing the rock, reminding us of embracing the hard places.

I speak for the standing ones, the trees. We grow tall, we grow straight. We are the spine of the earth, reaching deep with our roots and stretching tall to the sky, connecting the two. They teach us to do likewise.

I speak for the hawk and for the eagle. I sound my barbaric cry over the rooftops of the world. And I warn that my extinction is a sign for all of us to be concerned about our survival.

(After reading these examples, the Guide will say:) Let us begin now to call in the Sacred Hoop of All Beings. Look into the flame of life and speak for the members of the earth, so that our Mother may enter the New Time, the Good Time, the Greening Time. (Ten to fifteen minutes)

PART SEVEN: BURYING THE HATCHETS
AND PLANTING THE TREE OF PEACE.

(The Guide will hand out pieces of paper and ask the participants to make small hatchets out of the paper. The participants should write or draw on the hatchets those things that give rise in them to thoughts of conflict and negativity: old grudges, hatreds, negative holdings about others or themselves. When this is done, the Guide and the participants, accompanied by the sound of the drum, carry the tree and shovel to the spot where the tree will be planted. Each participant takes a turn with the shovel to help in the digging. When the hole is deep enough, the Guide will say:) Now will each of you, one by one, place your hatchet of hates and grudges into this hole, knowing that this symbolic act consecrates your desire to be rid of these thoughts and patterns of behavior. Know too that the great force of nature will turn these leavings into compost and make them the basis for good and growing things. If you need to speak aloud what you are burying, please do so as you place your hatchets in this good soil.

(After all have buried their hatchets, the Guide will invite participants to help plant the Tree of Peace over the hatchets, saying something like the following, but letting the words come from her heart:)

Let us now plant together this little pine tree, symbolic of the Great Tree of Peace. As we do so, we call upon the Spirit of the Peacemaker, of Hiawatha, of the Peace Woman Jigonhsasee, and of the one who became peaceful, Tadodaho, to bless our efforts and bring peace into our hearts and into our lives. May this little tree of peace grow into a great tree of peace and spread its roots far into the world.

(The Guide will invite the other participants to offer their wishes and blessings for the little tree. When this is completed, the Guide will say:) Let us now conclude this ceremonial first by thanking the powers of the directions. (All turn to each of the directions and give thanks.) Now let us end our journey together by speaking the sacred words drawn from the Navaho prayer of the Beautyway. Would you repeat after me these words of the prayer:

> With beauty behind me may I walk (Repeat)
> With beauty above me may I walk. (Repeat)
> With beauty below me may I walk. (Repeat)
> With beauty all around me may I walk. (Repeat)
> As one who is long life and happiness may I walk. (Repeat)
> In beauty it is finished. (Repeat)
> In beauty it is finished. (Repeat)

NOTES

1 John G. Niehardt, *Black Elk Speaks: Being the Life Story of a Holy Man of the Oglala Sioux as Told Through John G. Niehardt (Flaming Rainbow)* (Lincoln: University of Nebraska Press, 1972, 1989), pp. 198–200.

2 Joseph Epes Brown, *The Sacred Pipe: Black Elk's Account of the Seven Rites of the Oglala Sioux* (Middlesex, England: Penguin Books, 1953).

3 Joanna Macy offers a similar ceremony, which she calls "The Council of All Beings."

STEPS IN THE MANUAL
FOR THE PEACEMAKER

T he steps in the process of becoming the Peacemaker reflect the work of the chapters of this book and the processes to quicken this becoming given at the close of each chapter.

Step One: **Embrace the Open Moment,** recognizing that each moment may be experienced as a new birth and as a spectacularly open time, when what we do can make a difference to whether the human race grows or dies.

Process One: **Do the Impossible.** As Deganawidah was able to float a stone canoe as proof that his words were true, so may we work from our inmost truth, leaving outmoded beliefs about ourselves behind in order to accomplish tasks and projects we may feel are impossible.

Step Two: **Embrace the True Message,** as the hunters on the shore and the Erie woman who fed the warriors were willing to embrace the Good News of Peace and Power that Deganawidah brought. When you hear a good message, respond wholeheartedly, "I take hold of it; it is good."

Process Two: **Stop Nourishing the Toxic Raiders,** both within and without, who destroy your peace of mind and make you less effective as a bringer of peace to others.

Step Three: **Welcome the Consciousness that Carries the Mind of the Maker.** In that creative matrix, find symbols and metaphors that are earthy and real to help carry the potency of peace, as Deganawidah used the image of the Longhouse to share his vision with the tribes.

Process Three: **Become a Partner of Creation.** Discover ways that allow you to enter the Mind of the Maker—to be refreshed, to use your whole brain/mind to find new solutions to old problems, as well as to reveal your points of access to Great Mind.

Step Four: **Go Toward the Sunrise,** by being willing to encounter people and things which may be frightening, as Deganawidah deliberately sought the house of the cannibal.

Process Four: Be willing to **See the True Face** of the other, to hear the deeper story, since doing so often leads us to a soul ally. Do not be afraid to **Admit Your Handicaps.** When we see everyone as a deep ally in the soul's journey, we find colleagues whose skills complement our own, as Hiawatha's skill as an orator complemented Deganawidah's difficulty in speaking.

Step Five: **Risk the Fall into a New Form.** Accept the fact that your truth will be tested again and again, and never give up working one-to-one, or group-to-group, to spread the Good News of Peace and Power.

Process Five: When others disagree with you, stand for what you know to be true, realizing that others may be won to your cause by your willingness to **Hack Away the Tree of Falsehood.** Be willing even to fall—or fail—into a richer understanding of your truth.

Step Six: **Lift Grief** wherever you find it, by encouraging those who suffer to harvest the richness of their life and loves by telling of them in a ritualized manner, as Deganawidah heard Hiawatha's heart cry and responded with words of condolence and quickening.

Process Six: **Allow Your Griefs to Reveal their Full Story.** Create the equivalent of strands of wampum to hold your life's deep story. Be willing to tell that story and allow each telling to enrich and add new dimensions to the glory of your life's experiences.

Step Seven: **Work with a Larger Circle of Allies,** whose thoughts and concerns add perspective and energy to your ideas. With the help of these allies, **Heal the Crooked One,** as Deganawidah and Hiawatha healed Tadodaho with ceremony, song, persuasion, and vision.

Process Seven: **Invest the Crooked One with a Higher Usefulness,** as Deganawidah and Hiawatha made Tadodaho the keeper of the council fire. Embody as well the power of Hiawatha, He Who Combs, to straighten the crookedness which persistent and debilitating lies create in your profession.

Step Eight: **Meet in Councils of Cooperation and Cocreation.** Create new forms of authentically democratic community based on the desire for justice, health, and spiritual power.

Process Eight: **Plant and Nurture the Great Tree of Peace.** Never cease to give thanks for the Sacred Hoop of Life. Listen for the vision and need encoded in dreams. Be willing to bury the hatchet of war thoughts. And above all, never give up.

MUSICAL SELECTIONS

The following are listings of Native American music or music inspired by Native American themes. Environmental sound recordings are also included. Those selections marked by an asterisk are ones that we have found to be particularly effective for processes and exercises used in this book. Tapes and CD's of this music, especially the marked selections, are available from:

Wind Over The Earth, Inc.
1980 Eighth Street, Ste. F
Boulder, CO 80302
(800) 726–0847

Another valuable source for materials for working with the Manual for the Peacemaker is the Bear Tribe Catalogue. It is filled with wonderful items relating to Native American culture: books, drums, rattles, smudge sticks, and tapes of Native American songs and dances. The Bear Tribe catalogue can be requested from Wind Over the Earth, or directly from

Bear Tribe Medicine Society
P.O. Box 9167
Spokane, WA 99209

It is also important that you or your group have at least one drum for doing the exercises. A Native American drum is always preferable for carrying the spirit and the sound of the Peacemaker processes.

Bryan Akipa, *Flute Player* (AKI-MS001)
James Bilagody, *Beauty Ways* (BIL-SOAR132)

Black Lodge Singers, *Pow Wow Highway Songs* (POW-SOAR125)

Sharon Burch, *The Blessing Ways* (YAZ-CR533)

Sharon Burch, *Yazzie Girl* (YAZ-CR534)

*Cathedral Lake Singers, *Pow-Wow Wow Songs I* (CAT-SOAR116)

Cathedral Lake Singers, *Pow-Wow Wow Songs II* (CAT-SOAR122)

*Robert Tree Cody, *Young Eagles Flight* (YOU-CR533)

*Coyote Oldman, *Compassion* (COM-CO7)

Coyote Oldman, *In Medicine River* (INM-CO5T)

*Coyote Oldman, *Landscape* (LAN-C03)

*Coyote Oldman, *Nightforest* (NIG-C01)

*Coyote Oldman, *Tear of the Moon* (TEA-CO2)

Coyote Oldman, *Thunderchord* (LAN-CO4)

T. Crawford & P. Stavenjord, *Guardian Spirits* (CRA-C&S001)

Dik Darnell, *Following The Circle* (DAR-EC70014)

Dik Darnell, *Voice Of The Four Winds* (DAR-EC70024)

Dik Darnell, *Winter Solstice Ceremony* (DAR-EC70034)

Denean, *Fire Prayer* (DEN-EC71014)

Denean, *The Weaving* (DEN-EMC7102)

*Brooke Medicine Eagle, *A Gift Of Song* (EAG-BME4)

*Brooke Medicine Eagle, *Drumming The Heartbeat* (EAG-BME2)

*Brooke Medicine Eagle, *For My People* (EAG-BME1)

Brooke Medicine Eagle, *Grandmother Wisdom* (EAG-BME12)

Brooke Medicine Eagle, *Healing Through Ritual Action* (EAG-BME3)

Brooke Medicine Eagle, *Visions Speaking* (EAG-BME11)

William Eaton, *Wisdom Tree* (WIS-CR7009)

*Elk Nation Singers, *Spirit Drum* (ELK-NSS1014)

*Environment Series, *Environments 1 - Slow Ocean* (SYN-SC99001)

*Environment Series, *Environments 9 - Heartbeat* (SYN-SC99009)

*Environment Series, *Environments 10 - Gentle Rain* (SYN-SC99010)

*Gene Groeschel, *Hawk Eyes Dreaming* (GRO-GG001)

Guy & Allen, *Peyote Canyon* (PEY-SOAR129)

Ben Tavera King, *Coyote Moon* (KIN-R479331)

Ben Tavera King, *Desert Dreams* (KIN-OZ40725)

Ben Tavera King, *Themes of Passion* (THE-TT107)

Ben Tavera King & J. Reyes, *Turquoise Trail* (TUR-TT105)

Ben Tavera King, *Visions & Encounters* (VIS-TT113)

*Kevin Locke, *Dream Catcher* (DRE-EB2696)

Kevin Locke, *Lakota Love Songs* (LOC-KL001)

*Kevin Locke, *The Seventh Direction* (LOC-KL002)

*Medicine Wheel, *On Wings of Song and Robert Gass* (SHM-1015)

Mesa Music Consort, *Ceremonies of Dusk and Dawn* (CER-TT112)

*Mesa Music Consort, *Medicine Flutes* (MES-TT116)

Robert Mirabal, *Something In The Fog* (MIR-YAC002)

Robert Mirabal, *Sys-To-Le* (MIR-YAC001)

Robert Mirabal, *Warriors* (MIR-YAC003)

Davis Mitchell, *Navajo Singer Sings For You* (NAV-SOAR107)

Carlos Nakai & Wm. Eaton, *Ancestral Voices* (ANC-CR7010)

Carlos Nakai & Jackalope, *Boat People* (JAC-CR7003)

*Carlos Nakai, *Canyon Trilogy* (CAN-CR610)

Carlos Nakai & Wm. Eaton, *Carry The Gift* (CAR-CR7006)

Carlos Nakai, *Changes* (CHA-CR615)

Carlos Nakai, *Cycles* (CYC-CR614)

Carlos Nakai, *Desert Dance* (DES-CH3033)

*Carlos Nakai, *Earth Spirit* (EAR-CR612)

Carlos Nakai, *Emergence* (EME-CR609)

Carlos Nakai & Jackalope, *Jackalope* (JAC-CR7001)

Carlos Nakai, *Journeys* (JOU-CR613)

Carlos Nakai & James Demars, *Spirit Horses* (SPI-CR7014)

Carlos Nakai, *Sundance Season* (SUN-CH13024)

Carlos Nakai & Wm. Eaton, *Tracks We Leave* (TRA-CR7008)

Carlos Nakai & Jackalope, *Weavings* (WEA-CR7002)

*Native Flute Ensemble, *Enchanted Canyons* (ENC-TT103)
Native Flute Ensemble, *Gathering of Shamen* (GAT-TT119C)
Native Flute Ensemble, *Native Flute Collection* (NAT-TT111)
*Native Flute Ensemble, *Ritual Mesa* (RIT-TT101)
*Native Flute Ensemble, *Temple Of The Dream Jaguar* (TEM-TT108)
Nature Recordings, *Dawn & Dusk/Mountain Stream* (ENV-NR18)
Nature Recordings, *Songbirds Of Spring* (ENV-NR007)
Billie Nez, *Peyote Songs From Navaholand* (PEY-SOAR114)
Cornel Pewewardy, *Spirit Journey* (SPI-SOAR140)
John Rainer, *Songs of Ind. Flute I* (RAI-RW001)
John Rainer, *Songs of Ind. Flute II* (RAI-RW002)
Rainmaker, *Distant Thunder* (RAI-CR001)
Jessita Reyes, *Coyote Love Medicine* (COY-TT102)
Jessita Reyes & Grupo Yaq, *Deer Dancer* (DEE-TT110)
Jessita Reyes, *Seasons Of The Eagle* (SEA-TT106)
Sampler Soar, *Solo Flights* (SOL-SOAR124)
Perry Silverbird, *Blessing Way* (SIL-CH13046)
Rueben Silverbird, *The World In Our Eyes* (SIL-CH14040)
Douglas Spotted Eagle, *Ah-K' Pah-Zah* (AK-SOAR00)
Douglas Spotted Eagle, *Canyon Speak* (CAN-SOAR117)
Douglas Spotted Eagle, *Human Rites* (HUM-SOAR102)
Douglas Spotted Eagle, *Legend Of The Flute Boy* (LEG-SOAR115)
Douglas Spotted Eagle, *Sacred Feelings* (SAC-SOAR109)
Douglas Spotted Eagle, *Stand At The Center* (STA-SOAR101)
Various Artists, *65th Inter Tribal Ceremony* (VAR-IT001)
Various Artists, *Gathering/Nations Pow Wow* (VAR-SOAR133)
*Various Artists, *Honor The Earth Pow Wow* (VAR-RY0199)
Various Artists, *Navajo Songs . . . De Chelly* (VAR-NW80406)
Various Artists, *Pow Wow Songs Plains Indians* (VAR-NW80343)
Georgia Wettlin-Larsen, *Songs Of The People* (SON-CR4003)

SELECTED BIBLIOGRAPHY

Arrien, Angeles. *The Four Fold Way: Walking the Paths of the Warrior, Teacher, Healer and Visionary*. San Francisco: Harper SanFrancisco, 1993.

Basic Call to Consciousness. Mohawk Nation. Via Roosevelttown, New York: Akwesasne Notes, 1978.

Brown, Joseph Epes. *The Sacred Pipe: Black Elk's Account of the Seven Rites of the Oglala Sioux*. Middlesex, England: Penguin Books, 1953.

———.*The Spiritual Legacy of the American Indians*. New York: Crossroad, 1982.

Campbell, Joseph. *Historical Atlas of World Mythology*. Vol. 1: *The Way of the Animal Powers*. Vol. 2: *The Way of the Seeded Earth*. New York: Harper & Row, 1988, 1989.

Carey, Ken. *The Return of the Bird Tribes*. San Francisco: HarperSanFrancisco, 1991.

Cohen, Felix. "Americanizing the White Man." *American Scholar* 21:2 (1952).

Converse, Harriet M. *Myths and Legends of the New York Iroquois*. Albany, New York: State University Press, 1974.

Cornplanter, Jesse J. *Legends of the Longhouse*. Port Washington, New York: Ira J. Friedman, 1963.

Exiled in the Land of the Free: Democracy, Indian Nations, and the U.S. Constitution. Edited by Oren R. Lyons and John C. Mohawk. Santa Fe, N. Mex.: Clear Light Publishers, 1992.

Fenton, William N. "Iroquois Indian Folklore," *Journal of American Folklore* 60 (1947): 383–97.

———. "The Lore of the Longhouse: Myth, Ritual and Red Power." *Anthropological Quarterly* 48 (1975): 131–47.

———. "Seth Newhouse's Traditional History and Constitution of the Iroquois Confederacy." *Proceedings of the American Philosophical Society* 93 (1949): 141–58.

Fiske, Stephen Longfellow. *The Art of Peace: A Personal Manual on Peacemaking and Creativity.* Limited edition, published by the author.

Franklin, Benjamin. "Remarks Concerning the Savages of North-America." In *Benjamin Franklin: Writings.* Edited by J. A. Leo Lemay. New York: The Library of America, 1987.

Gibson, John Arthur. "The Deganawidah Legend: A Tradition of the Founding of the League of the Five Iroquois Tribes," as told to J. N. B. Hewitt, ed., Abram Charles, John Buck, Sr., and Joshua Buck (1900–1914) from the legend recorded in the 1890's. Translated by William N. Fenton and Simeon Gibson. Smithsonian Institution: *Bureau of American Ethnology Archives* 1517C (1941).

Graymont, Barbara. *The Iroquois.* New York: Chelsea House Press, 1988.

Hale, Horatio. *The Iroquois Book of Rites.* Philadelphia: D. G. Brinton, 1883.

Henry, Thomas R. *Wilderness Messiah: The Story of Hiawatha and the Iroquois.* New York: William Sloane Associates, 1955.

Hertzberg, Hazel W. *The Great Tree and the Longhouse: The Culture of the Iroquois*. New York: Macmillan, 1966.

Highwater, Jamake. *The Primal Mind: Vision and Reality in Indian America*. New York: New American Library, 1983.

Howard, Helen A. "Hiawatha: Co-Founder of an Indian United Nations." *Journal of the West* 10: 428–38.

I Become Part of It: Sacred Dimensions in Native American Life. Edited by D. M. Dooling and Paul Jordan-Smith. San Francisco: HarperSanFrancisco, 1992.

Indian Roots of American Democracy. Edited by Jose Barreiro. Ithaca, New York: AKWE:KON Press, Cornell University, 1992.

Jennings, Francis. *The Ambiguous Iroquois Empire*. New York: W. W. Norton, 1984.

Johansen, Bruce E. *Forgotten Founders: Benjamin Franklin, the Iroquois and the Rationale for the American Revolution*. Ipswich, Mass.: Gambit, Inc., 1982.

Macy, Joanna. *Despair and Personal Power in the Nuclear Age*. Philadelphia: New Society Publishing, 1983.

———. *World as Lover, World as Self*. Berkeley, Cal.: Parallax Press, 1991.

Mails, Thomas E. *Secret Native American Pathways: A Guide to Inner Peace*. Tulsa, Okla.: Council Oak Books, 1991.

Matthiessen, Peter. *Indian Country*. New York: Viking, 1984.

———. *In the Spirit of Crazy Horse*. New York: Penguin Books, 1992.

McFadden, Steven. *Ancient Voices, Current Affairs*. Sante Fe, N. Mex.: Bear & Company, 1992.

McGaa, Ed (Eagle Man). *Rainbow Tribe: Ordinary People Journeying on the Red Road*. San Francisco: Harper SanFrancisco, 1992.

Morgan, Lewis Henry. *League of the Ho-De-No-Sau-Nee or Iroquois*. New Haven, Conn: Human Relations Area Files, 1954.

Newhouse, Seth (Dayodekane). "Constitution of the Confederacy by Dekanawidah." Translated by J. N. B. Hewitt (1937) from the oral telling by Newhouse in 1897. Smithsonian Institution: *Bureau of American Ethnology Archives* 3490.

Niehardt, John G. *Black Elk Speaks: Being the Life Story of a Holy Man of the Oglala Sioux as Told Through John G. Niehardt (Flaming Rainbow)*. Lincoln, Nebr.: University of Nebraska Press, 1972, 1989.

The Sacred Path. Edited by John Bierhorst. New York: William Morrow, 1983.

Sams, Jamie and Nitsch, Twylah. *Other Council Fires Were Here Before Ours*. San Francisco: HarperSanFrancisco, 1991.

Schmookler, Andrew Bard. *Out of Weakness: Healing the Wounds That Drive Us to War*. New York: Bantam, 1988.

Snyder, Gary. *Turtle Island*. New York: New Directions Press, 1969.

Storm, Hyemeyohsts. *Seven Arrows*. New York: Ballantine Books, 1972.

Sturtevant, William.*The Native Americans, Indigenous People of North America*. New York: Smithmark Publishers, 1991.

Sun Bear. *The Medicine Wheel: Earth Astrology*. New York: Prentice Hall Press, 1980.

Vecsey, Christopher. *Imagine Ourselves Richly: Mythic Narratives of North American Indians*. San Francisco: Harper SanFrancisco, 1991.

Wall, Steve and Arden, Harvey. *Wisdomkeepers: Meetings with Native American Spiritual Elders*. Hillsboro, Ore.: Beyond Words Publishing, 1990.

Wallace, Anthony F. C. *The Death and Rebirth of the Seneca*. New York: Knopf, 1970.

———. "Dreams and Wishes of the Soul: A Type of Psychoanalytic Theory among the Seventeenth Century Iroquois." *American Anthropologist* 60 (1958): 234–48.

———. "The Dekanawideh Myth Analyzed as the Record of a Revitalization Movement." *Ethnohistory* 5 (1958): 118–30.

Wallace, Paul A. W. *The White Roots of Peace*. Philadelphia: University of Pennsylvania Press, 1946, reprinted 1986.

Weatherford, Jack. *Indian Givers*. New York: Fawcett Columbine, 1988.

———. *Native Roots: How the Indians Nourished America*. New York: Crown, 1991.

Ywahoo, Dhyani. *Voices of Our Ancestors: Cherokee Teachings from the Wisdom Fire*. Boston: Shambhala, 1987.